# Scholarships for Indian Citizens

# Table of Contents

Table of Contents ............................................................................................ 2

Disclaimer ....................................................................................................... 3

About the Author ............................................................................................ 5

Free Gift Included ........................................................................................... 6

Introduction .................................................................................................... 8

Tips on how to carry out an Effective search for Scholarship ..................... 14

List of Scholarships for Studying in the USA ................................................ 43

List of Scholarships for Studying in UK and Europe .................................... 94

List of Scholarships for Studying in Australia ............................................ 134

List of Scholarships for Studying in Canada .............................................. 165

World Bank / International Loans (Other Global organizations) that give Education Loans to Developing Economies ............................................... 188

Reliable sources for loans in India ............................................................. 195

Developed countries (with GDP per capita > $25000) with lowest education cost ............................................................................................................... 208

Conclusion ................................................................................................... 224

## Disclaimer

Copyright © 2016

All Rights Reserved

All rights reserved. This book or any portion thereof may not be reproduced or used in any manner whatsoever without the express written permission of the publisher except for the use of brief quotations in a book review.

The information in this book is intended to provide useful information on the topics mentioned. Great care has been taken to ensure that the details in this book are accurate and up-to-date. However, the authors do not assume responsibility for any incorrect information that may be in this book. This includes information that is out of date.

# About the Author

Abhishek Kumar is a Georgia Institute of Technology Masters' Thesis graduate in Mechanical Engineering. He has worked for five years in Chicago, as a Design Engineer at Continental Brazil, and as a Software Developer at Engineous Software in Atlanta.

He has gained valuable experience living on four separate continents and travelling across the world over the past decade, mostly as a student. He is dedicated to sharing his experiences in travel and career planning with other students through eBooks, blogs and products. Tired of the corporate life, he has now moved back to his hometown to pursue his interests as an entrepreneur and author. He has written several books geared towards helping students with their careers and with affordable global travel.

He also has a blog on career advice at:

www.indianstudyabroad.com

## Free Gift Included

As part of our dedication to help you succeed in your career, we have sent you a free interview preparation template. This is the "30 Minute Interview Preparation Template. This is a quick list of questions that you can answer before any job interview to ensure that you have done your research on the company, and on your fit for the company. It should take you no more than 30 minutes to complete the day before the interview.

Click on the link below to get your free template.

http://30minuteinterviewpreptemplate.gr8.com

# Introduction

Studying in a foreign university in a developed country has long been seen as a gateway to a better standard of living. Increased knowledge, along with the resulting increase in job opportunities, are both important factors. Universities in Europe, the United States, Australia, and Canada expose their students to people from all different corners of the globe. Students are able to learn to work with people from different cultural backgrounds and pick up skills that will make them more employable globally. Obviously, it is important that they work hard once they get there and make the right decisions; but they definitely have an opportunity for a better life.

However, people from India looking to study abroad have several obstacles that they need to overcome. The biggest burden is the financial one. People from upper middle class and rich families can afford the fees needed for the high grade of education, but everyone else must scramble for their chance. There is the opportunity to apply for graduate research and graduate teaching assistantships, but those who are not able to get these positions must rely on loans taken from Indian banks at very high interest rates. Given the high cost of foreign education and low wages at home, it is almost impossible for graduates to pay off their loans with an Indian salary. So understandably, students are under significant pressure to get jobs in their countries of schooling. This can be particularly difficult as most jobs cater to those with local citizenship.

If students are debt free at the end of their university program, it gives them a lot of options in their careers. They are able to take risks in their professional careers, start businesses, travel, and spend money to improve their local economy. It makes a tremendous difference for them to have the opportunity of spending the best years of their lives following their dreams, rather than just contributing to the economy by slowly paying off their debts.

From my personal experiences with study abroad scholarships, I learned that most of the scholarships that are available to students require citizenship or permanent residence in the country in question. At Georgia Tech, there were plenty of scholarships available to local residents of Georgia, USA; and most of the local students could cover their entire tuitions with scholarships. The international students were left hanging. In addressing this issue, our team looked at several programs, both in India and the developed countries. There are scholarships in the USA, Australia, and Europe that are specifically for students from developing countries to help educate their countries' workforces. There are also scholarships awarded by private and public organizations in India that are exclusively for Indian citizens. Several universities provide their own scholarships as well. This book is a directory featuring several of the most prominent scholarships that might be available to benefit you in your studies, making an immense difference in your life. Many students have demonstrated great potential in their study life but lack the resources to fund their education. Scholarships provide these students with the opportunity to pursue their studies. They can then go on to develop careers in fields that they are passionate about, enhancing the level of expertise within their nation.

The objective of this book is to simplify the process for Indian students looking for scholarship opportunities to further their education. You will learn detailed information about scholarship opportunities that are suitable for the academic needs of Indian students, thereby providing you with higher chances of qualification. There are numerous lists of institutions, organizations, foundation and other bodies offering scholarship opportunities that are ideal for Indian students. Whether you are seeking undergraduate, graduate, post graduate, doctoral or PhD scholarships, you will get access to a variety of opportunities that better addresses your particular situation and academic interests. Each entry contains all the relevant information that the applicant may need. This includes the name of the scholarship, amount, eligibility, deadline for submitting applications, and website address where you can find additional information. Countless people have lost money to scammers who take advantage of students' lack of knowledge regarding what is required for their application to be considered. The information shared in this book will give you more insight into the requirements for the featured awards, which can be incredibly useful when completing your application or even researching other options that are not covered here.

It is very important to note that the requirements are different for each institution, so not all of the information will apply in each circumstance; but by understanding what the individual requirements are for different institutions, you will be able to prepare yourself appropriately. This will help ensure that you have the appropriate qualifications to guarantee your consideration for the award in question, eliminating the time you may otherwise spend applying for scholarships for which you would not qualify.

As a bonus for downloading this book, you will receive an extra chapter describing how to carry out an effective search for a desired scholarship, along with tips on writing a winning proposal. You will also learn how to avoid being scammed, along with other beneficial insights into the process. I highly recommend that you read the entire book rather than skipping sections, as you may not otherwise know what best suits your academic needs. I wish you success in your academic journey! Note: All application deadlines in this book are for 2016-17 season; and the dates may change for the years following 2016-2017.

# Tips on how to carry out an Effective search for Scholarship

The process of searching for appropriate scholarship opportunities can be quite competitive given the huge number of students that are applying for the scholarships. Before you apply for any scholarship opportunity it is advisable that you consider if it can appropriately meet your financial needs. If that is not possible then you can continue to carry on with your search until you get that which meets your academic funding needs.

**Myths about applying to top-tier universities such as Stanford or Georgia Tech**

There are myths associated with every facet of life. Whenever there is a myth, there lies the ignorance – lack of knowledge – a void compensated by filling it with unfounded beliefs and superstitions. Myths block you from reasoning. They prevent you from seeing the horizon of your vision and thus obstruct you from pursuing your goals. To help you clear these obstructions so that you can properly see your vision, we highlight the common myths and help you debunk them:

## Myth 1: You can't qualify for scholarships to top Universities

**Fact:** Competition to get into a top university is high. However, keep in mind that if you get in; you will be always impress any employer, person, university with the name of you graduation university. You have an advantage in life. It is definitely worth a shot. Most top universities do have funding assistance programs for those in need. So, if you are able to get in, you will be eligible to apply for those programs. Also, your chances of getting an external scholarship increase once they hear your university name.

## Myth 2: Grades alone matters

**Fact:** Most universities offer a scholarship, not really because they are unable to get those with good grades, but for different reasons. The education system itself and the thousands of applications ensure that they get people with the right grades. However, having the right grades does not necessarily mean that you have the right passion. It does not necessarily mean that you are going to bring the biggest impact to the world once you graduate. Other factors like your scholarship essay, extracurricular activities, in-person interview etc. may be used to gauge your level of passion for your field.

**Myth 3: Expensive college is a better one**

Many people mistakenly believe that expensive is better. Many students have not been spared of this false belief. Expensive is not always better! There are underlying factors can make something more expensive while still not better than the cheaper options. These include:

- Economic costs – Cost of running a university varies from one region to another. A purely urban university would be costlier to run than a university in a rural setup. On the other hand, a University of the same standard and quality would be more expensive to run in California than in Georgia. Thus, based on cost, you might be mistaken to think that the university in California is better.

- Misinformation – Marketing can easily create hype. Thus, universities that extensively market themselves could create a misguided impression that they are the best there is in the market. More often than not, they are more expensive than those that do not market extensively. This is because, first, they have to recoup their marketing cost in form of higher fees. Second, due to them being pricey, they have to advertise extensively to compensate for the opportunity lost by those who are turned away by the high fees.

- Price discrimination – If a university wants to appeal to the wealthy, it is going to charge exorbitant fees so that it discourages the poor from joining. This will create a class university for the rich, some of whom would be disadvantaged if grades were a strict criterion.

## Do the calculation about how much you will make once you graduate

Education is an investment. Like any other investment, you need to factor in what you are likely going to earn, not only as compensation for your cost incurred but also reward for your ingenuity.

The best way to arrive at the minimum you expect as your reward is to compute the opportunity cost of your higher education. From your opportunity cost, you can then be able to top-up with your desired premium (which could also be the difference between opportunity cost and the market rate of reward).

## Tips for Scholarship Application

Below are some of the tips that you can find helpful in your search for a scholarship:

- **Start the search process early**

Many people miss on scholarship opportunities not because they don't meet the requirements, but they wait until late to begin the search process. Each scholarship has a deadline date for submitting the application and it is vital that you carry out your research well and get to submit your applications in good time. Submitting the applications early will also give you sufficient time to search for numerous scholarships and apply for the ones that seems ideal for your academic needs.

- **Don't Be Afraid to Apply to Other Scholarships During a Waiting Period**

When it comes to obtaining money for college, nothing should get in the way of another chance and a lot of people lose out on scholarships they might have won because they didn't apply to others as they were waiting for the "special" scholarship. Unless the rules specifically state that you cannot apply to other scholarships while you wait for approval as some of scholarship providers will do, there is no reason for you not to seek additional scholarships while you wait for approval. Many times, additional scholarships help carry any extra load you may have when your primary scholarship simply won't cover it.

A great example of this is the Pell Grant many enjoy in the United States, which normally doesn't fully cover students for the full costs of college. Poetry competitions or other avenues are used to acquire an additional scholarship to pay for the remaining costs because applying for college and working at a job is often not immediately applicable to American students due to the sheer amount of time that college requires. Many American students go to a college that's not local to their city. Additionally, it also works as a fall back if your primary scholarship is rejected further down the road due to some unforeseen complication such as a billing confliction or an extended medical leave. These backup scholarships serve as a fall back net to cover some of the costs while you attempt to reinstate your primary scholarship.

- **Not All Scholarships Are Listed Online**

As remarkable as today's technology is, some organizations prefer to reserve their scholarships for those that plan to be in the city. If you have a list of colleges that you want to attend, and you know that, if you get a scholarship, you will be going to that college, then you want to call the college guidance counselor to see if you can get any scholarships in the local area that are not available online. Many of the scholarships that are online will receive a heavy amount of competition while those in the local area of the schools that you want to go to will receive significantly less competition, especially if they're offline. Not only do these types of scholarships have low competition but they also have short lifespans, which means you can try them multiple times, earn them when you need some extra money to pick up the slack, and apply them throughout the seasons rather than once every year like many high competition scholarships.

This list also includes scholarships that are exclusive; scholarships that require your part inside of an organization. Free Mason groups and some religious organizations that you may be affiliated with without knowing it could have scholarships that are exclusive and only known to participating members in the area. These scholarships can even be better than scholarships you're looking at getting or scholarships you may already have because many of these exclusive membership scholarships come with continuing payments. Looking for offline scholarships could lead you to a treasure trove of scholarships that you would not have had access to otherwise.

- **Network the Difficult Scholarships**

Just like the job positions that you will eventually look for, networking should be a part of your agenda whenever you are seeking out scholarships. You can try to network with the people who grant the scholarships. Simply send them a message saying that you are interested in a topic they may be interested in. Do not mention the scholarship at all and induce a conversation that gets them to be your friend. This might favor you in the scholarship competition over other competitors. This is a very rare trait amongst people because many people don't do more than simply send in an application. Networking is great for getting the job that you want, the raise that you want, and especially the scholarship in most circumstances. The best situation in which you can utilize networking is if the scholarship is granted by more than one person because if the scholarship is granted by one person then they will automatically be suspicious of you when you send them an email. If you only send one person out of ten an email, they are not likely to be suspicious of you and they are more likely to reach out their hands in friendship. Additionally, if you manage to not get the scholarship that you were going for but you retain the friendship that you made in the attempt of getting the scholarship, this can serve you later on down the line if you're looking for a job, if you are looking for a way into a very difficult industry, and will generally help you if you have any questions that your school is unable to answer because the people who administer the scholarships often have to know a lot more than the counselors found in schools since the counselors primarily have to only pay attention to what applies to that school.

- **Secondary Scholarships and New Scholarships**

Secondary scholarships are not the same as additional scholarships or primary scholarships because secondary scholarships only activate when you lose a scholarship. These are very rare and somewhat hard to find for all regions, but they do exist and they are extremely helpful if you need a scholarship to take over if another scholarship fails. While the Pell Grant isn't normally a secondary item that serves specifically as a secondary scholarship, it can act as one. A person that applies for a Pell Grant has access to that Pell Grant for up to a year to apply it to anything that they need and so if their scholarship fails during that year that the Pell Grant has been given to them, they are able to utilize the Pell Grant to recover from their losses. This is an excellent example of what a secondary scholarship does and why you should obtain at least one for every year that you attend college.

This brings me to my next point, which is that you shouldn't solely rely on a singular scholarship because anything could happen to that scholarship during the 4 to 8 years that you're inside of a college. This is why you should always be on the lookout for new scholarships that you can apply for because even if you don't use it, it's great to have scholarships on the side just in case. New scholarships come out all the time and their requirements change all the time, which means that people are less likely to find them. They either obtained the scholarship that they needed before it came out or the scholarship is so new that it's difficult to find. When new scholarships come onto the market, only those who consistently search for scholarships will be able to know that it's there and take advantage of it.

**How to write a winning proposal**

Writing a winning scholarship is has its own psychological aspects. You are more of a seller who must learn buyer psychology to induce demand. Every seller knows that just being in the market is not sufficient. This is the same concept when it comes to scholarship market.

## The psychology behind writing a winning scholarship essay - stand out

A scholarship essay is about uniquely positioning yourself, inviting your potential customer (scholarship provider) into your shop (your mind) and making a sales appeal (What you are offering, why you are the best, the unique benefit to the scholarship provider due to your candidature [that, achieving their mission through you]).

The following are key features that will make your scholarship essay standout:

- Distinctive style
- Unique insight
- Future aspirations

**Know your audience**

Before you start the writing process you should have a clear picture of the kind of audience you are writing for. When you understand the audience, you will figure out mentally what they may be looking out for and what can make them select your proposal from amongst a heap of equally well written proposals. Remember that having the qualifications alone is not enough. How you articulate your ideas on paper is quite vital as it is what gives the selection panel a clear picture of who you truly are and why you should be given a chance.

Get some insight on who is in the committee, whether they are PhD holders from different field, whether they represent Universities, Philanthropists, whether they are native English speakers and the countries they are from.

- **Make your introduction catchy and appealing**

When you are starting off with writing your proposal, remember the impact a good introductory statement can have on your entire proposal. Rehearse your writing until you are able to write an introduction that is catchy and appealing. A weak introduction might discredit you and deny you the funding even if the content of the essay seems ideal. Ensure that you get it right from the beginning, a quality introduction with great content.

- **Understand the goal of the organization giving the scholarship**

Scholarships provided by World Bank will have a different goal from that provided by Dalai Lama Foundation. Understand the goal clearly and tailor your proposal in a way that addresses how you can add value to their ultimate goal after you finish your college. If the goal of the scholarship is to educate students to improve conditions in developing countries, talk about your plans to use education to improve India. If the goal is to improve quality of research, talk about your ambitions to contribute to the relevant field.

- **Answer questions appropriately and make your proposal simple**

There are questions that you will be asked to answer, ensure that you avoid use of complicated terms that may not bring a clear meaning of what you are trying to express. Instead use words that are simple and addresses the question clearly. Speaking about obvious things and repeating yourself just to fill the space may create an impression that you have no clarity on what you have been asked.

- **Edit and proofread**

The best thing to do when it comes to editing and proofreading is to look for someone good at it to edit for you. It is hard to edit, and more so, thoroughly proofread your own work. This is because your brain is still in autocorrect mode. In this mode, the brain reads out the entire word by taking cues from the few characters of the word and extracting the complete word from your memory to read out. Thus, you are more likely to be reading from your own memory rather than from what you have already written.

## Unique insight

Make your essay personal and passionate. They are interested in you. Relate the question's theme to your past and present experiences. Also, relate it to how the scholarship is going to help you achieve a shared goal. A shared goal is that which both you and your scholarship provider intends to achieve through the scholarship.

## Future aspirations

Explain what your future would be with the scholarship. Figure yourself doing the things that the scholarship intends to get done. Manifest the vision of how the future should be once the shared goal is accomplished.

## 5 Examples of scholarship essays

There are varied types of essays depending on your scholarship, institution of learning and particular interest from scholarship provider.

The following are the five examples of scholarship essays that you could be asked to write:

1. Why should you be selected for this scholarship? Please describe in detail any leadership endeavors, community engagements and academic achievements that prove you deserve this scholarship.
2. What are your career goals and how will earning a degree from our University help you achieve those goals?
3. In no more than 500 words, please let us know you and your reasons for applying for this scholarship.
4. Describe an event in which you took leadership role and what you learned about yourself.
5. Narrate an experience that made a lasting impression on you and your life

**Scholarship Essay format**

Specifically, most scholarship providers specify their own formatting requirements. However, should there be no custom specification; the following general standard format applies:

**Spacing**: Double Spaced

**Font style**: Times New Roman

**Font Size**: 12 points

**Margins**: 1-inch margin, all-round

**The scholarship skeleton**

A scholarship essay has no specific skeleton. This is because most essay questions are custom and specific. However, it should have the following flow:

- **Personal Details:** You need to identify yourself. Sometimes you may be provided with a different form where you fill your personal details. However, if you are not provided with this, it is logical that you need to identify yourself as the owner of the essay. Thus, provide your name, telephone contact and/or Email.

- **Title:** Provide a title to your essay.

- **First paragraph:** This is an introduction paragraph – make a catchy introduction that will motivate and inspire the reader to read further. Let it set the foundation for your subsequent paragraphs.

- **Middle paragraphs:** These are point paragraphs – anchor each paragraph to a specific point and be able to elaborate it.

- **Last paragraph:** This is a conclusion paragraph – conclude your essay by wrapping it up.

**SAMPLE ESSAY – PERSONAL STATEMENT**

In this essay, you are not being asked a particular question. You are simply required to make a personal statement to accompany your scholarship application. This is like a cover letter to an ordinary application. This is the most common type of scholarship essay.

To start-off, you need to make an outline. The outline will guide you on the flow of content and on what to consider in your essay.

<u>The outline</u>

1. Title: Personal Statement

2. Personal Details: Name, Telephone Contact, Email Address

3. Introduction

    - Name

    - Scholarship being applied for

4. Educational Objectives and Career Goals

    - Identify your major

    - Explain why you have chosen your major

    - Explain how this degree will impact on your career plans

- Elaborate on your future plans

5. Brief background

    - Give a narration about yourself

    - Explain your journey up to where you are today

    - State and give insight into your life values

    - Provide testimony that reflects your character and strengths

    - Prove what makes you unique and stand out from the rest, i.e. the extra-curricular activities – hobbies, voluntary work, etc.

6. Prove your need

    - State and prove why you need the scholarship

    - Show how it will make a difference to you

- If possible, show how it will enable you achieve the scholarship provider's mission

7. Conclusion

- Wrap up in a few sentences

- Tactically cite your vision should you win the scholarship and achieve the mission the scholarship intends to be achieved

- Show appreciation for the life you have lived, the achievements you have made leading you to be a potential candidate for the scholarship.

- Express gratitude for the opportunity granted to you

**SAMPLE ESSAY**

PERSONAL STATEMENT

Submitted by Chandika Gupta

Bose Scholarship Application

27th January, 2017

Email: chandi.gupta@mail.com

My name is Chandika Gupta. I completed my A-Levels at Sri Naga Senior School. I got a distinction in my core subjects – Math, Computer Science and Chemistry. Afterwards, I took a short course in auto engineering. It is with great esteem that I apply for your Bose Scholarship in science and engineering.

My career aspiration is to acquire a degree in automotive engineering. My career vision is to change the nature of transportation in India. I am certain that if I acquire a degree in automotive engineering from a top university, I will effectively cause the change I am seeking to make.

Having lived my entire life in a populated urban center, I see the need for change in the system. I was very lucky to have a great family that gave me a great education. My father drove me to school driving through rough traffic for 1 hour a day, through massive amounts of pollution. He then traveled another hour to work. We had the same problem on the way back. Being from a middle class family, this was a huge strain on both our health and resources. We both fell sick often and had to battle through school and work. I see the need for getting more sustainable forms of transportation to not only reduce our emissions but also improve our daily quality of life. I am very interested in progressing sustainable transportation solutions such as electric cars, and also in engineering of sustainable roads and highways; that can handle India's traffic and weather.

I believe I will be furthering Bose's legacy in science and technology. Being a top quality engineer, it will enable me to improve technology and help improve the country.. I am grateful that you have granted me this opportunity to apply for this scholarship, briefly share with you my life story, confide in you my dream and hope for a great future.

Thank you.

Yours Sincerely,

Chandika Gupta

**How to get letters of recommendation for scholarships**

Letter of recommendation is important to any scholarship application. The letter of recommendation helps the scholarship provider to:

- Get independent background information about you
- Authenticate some of your credentials
- Have a better insight about who you are

Thus, it is important to give a letter of recommendation the utmost attention it deserves.

The following steps would help you get your most deserving recommendation letter:

1. Find a qualified person who knows you well – Some scholarships providers could be specific on whom to recommend you. However, for recommendations on academic matters, your teacher, instructor or professor is in a better position to do that. For a recommendation on work-related matters (if any), the best recommender is your supervisor. For sports matters, your coach will do. For community and social matters, your pastor or mentor can do. Make sure that you ask for the recommendation in person.

2. Ask for the recommendation as early as possible – This allows you your recommender plenty of time before the deadline to prepare. Most scholarships grant you at least one month to do all these. To be on the safe side, have an

extra recommender just in case. If both successfully write a recommendation letter for you, choose one to present.

3. Provide and discuss important details about your scholarship with your recommender

4. Engage your recommender by reflecting on and sharing your goals, motivations and significant experiences that have shaped your life.

5. Provide your recommender with your CV or Resume

6. Waive your right to read the Recommendation – not to inhibit your recommender's freedom of conscience

7. Call to remind or send a reminder to your recommender some time in advance (probably a week) before your deadline. Make sure that everything is complete, thorough, and on time.

8. Follow up with a 'Thank You!' Note

# List of Scholarships for Studying in the USA

The United States of America is the top destinations for students looking for scholarship opportunities as they get a chance to access high quality education that is recognized world over. It is however important to note that most of the US scholarship opportunities are very competitive therefore one should try to effectively understand the requirements and be able to provide the required details correctly if they are to be considered for the opportunity to study in the United States.

Below are some of the scholarship opportunities that are available for study in the USA that Indian students can apply:

## 1. S. N. Bose Scholars Program

This scholarship is designed to provide Indian students with world class research facilities in the leading United States Institutions. The scholarship is provided to students pursuing Bachelor's degree or a Master's degree at a recognized high learning Institution in India. Students that are pursuing Engineering sciences, Computational Sciences, Atmospheric and Earth Sciences amongst other related courses are eligible for the scholarship.

**Scholarship Value**

The Scholarship takes covers the following:

- Living expenses and allowance
- Health Insurance
- Air Fare expenses

Eligibility

To be eligible for the award, applicants should be able to meet the following requirements:

- Should be Indian citizens that are currently pursuing a Bachelor's or Master's degree from a recognized higher learning institution in India.

- Applications in other fields other than the ones specified will not be accepted.
- Applications are also accepted through nominations or endorsements, institutions can nominate students that they feel deserve the scholarship.
- Application for the awards can be submitted online
- Deadline for submitting applications is 31st of October

More information can be accessed at: http://www.iusstf.org

## 2. J. N. Tata Scholarship

This award is available to students pursuing various courses with preference given to applicants admitted to College of Architecture, College of Engineering, College of Agriculture and Life Sciences. The scholarship is offered to students that have demonstrated financial need and have excellent academic results.

**Scholarship Value**

The value of scholarship may range between Rs. 50,000 to Rs. 400,000 for gift scholarship and loan scholarship may range between Rs 2,00,000/- to 10,00,000

**Eligibility**

To be eligible for the award, the applicant should meet the following requirements:

- Applicants should be Indian nationals that have graduated from a recognized university in India.
- Students who are in their final year in college and those waiting for results are also eligible to apply.
- Applicants should have admission letter from Cornell University.
- All applications should be submitted online and the deadline for submitting the application is 31st of March.

More information can be accessed from the website:

http://www.jntataendowment.org/loan-scholarship-process

## 3. Inlaks Shivdasani Foundation

Inlaks scholarships awards young Indian students who have demonstrated exceptional talent with the opportunity to improve their skills. They get to broaden their vision as they pursue their studies in some of the top universities in the US and the UK. There are two types of scholarships offered by the foundation, those that are University specific and program specific.

**Scholarship Value**

The value of the scholarship is not more than $100,000 and should cover tuition fees, living allowance and other costs. If at all the cost of studies exceeds $100,000 then students should show ability to cover the extra costs at the time of interview.

**Eligibility**

- The foundation does not give scholarships to students undertaking the following courses: Engineering, business studies, Computer science Business Studies, Fashion

Design, Public Health, Music and Field animation. However, scholarships for courses like Engineering and computer sciences can be offered to students pursuing the studies at the Imperial College, London. For music studies, only those students pursuing music applications will be considered for western classical singing degrees.

- Scholarships are available to Indian nationals who are living in India at the time of submitting application. Applicants are expected to be degree holders from a recognized University in India. The applicant must have been working in India for a period of two years after their undergraduate degree. Those having a postgraduate degree from outside India are not eligible for the scholarship.

- Applicants are advised to have prior admission to their preferred university before submitting applications for the scholarship including the course chosen. Applications from those who do not have admission from the preferred

University's or those with pending admission will not be considered. The admission should also be from a University that is top ranked.

- Applicants are required to be below 30 years by the time of submitting the application. Applicants who are already studying or those who have already undertaken the program abroad are not eligible.
- Any other award or grant and support from other sources for the proposed studies are considered a positive gesture by the foundation. Young people who are in employment are also encouraged to apply.
- Applicants are required to submit all the details of their proposed programs which may include a full breakdown of costs, travelling plans and agreement with the concerned institutions.
- There is requirement for proof that you are indeed an achiever. The foundation judges potential as much as it judges performance and it is not only what you have

achieved but what you are more likely to achieve with the help of the foundation.

- The applicant should be able to demonstrate that the kind of course chosen is appropriate and suits them well.
- Application forms can be accessed online and can also be obtained from the Foundation's offices in Mumbai. The application must be downloaded or taken from the offices and then filled and submitted through email or the available postal address
- The applicant should also provide the evidence of admission for a course or to a University and full details of the institutions financial requirement.
- Those candidates applying for courses in architecture, fine and applied arts and other related subjects should be able to provide about 10 samples of their work in a CD or DVD, the work will not be returned to the applicant.

- Applicant should provide evidence of achievement in extracurricular activities including photocopy of first and last page of passport.
- Submission of recommendation letters is not compulsory. However, the applicant can still submit them provided it's submitted with the application forms and in sealed envelopes. There should be a maximum of three recommendations.
- Copies of academic transcripts should not be included with the application form as they will be required during the final interview.
- The deadline for the application is 15th of April and applicants who shall have not received any communication by 1st of June should consider themselves unsuccessful.

All the information regarding the foundation can be accessed at: http://inlaksfoundation.org/scholarships/

## 4. Aga Khan Foundation International Scholarship Program

The Aga Khan foundation provides scholarships to a limited number of students who are mostly from developing countries and lack other means of financing their studies. The studies can be undertaken from anywhere in the world including the United States.

Priority is given to application requests for Masters' Level courses although PHD level courses are also considered.

**Scholarship Value**

Aga Khan Scholarship value is 50% of the amount payable is offered as grant and 50% is offered as loan repayable by the student after completion of studies. The total amount may vary depending on the college one is admitted to.

**Eligibility**

i. Priority is given to applicants from Bangladesh, India, Pakistan, and Egypt amongst other countries.

ii. The students are assisted with tuition fees and living expenses only and cost of travel is not included in the award. 50% of the award is considered as loan which is payable after completion of the study.

iii. Priority is given to students that are below 30 years of age.

iv. The deadline for International scholarship programs is 31 March (for 2017). The application form can be obtained from the local Aga Khan offices in January of each year.

v. Applicants should be ready to be interviewed by the local scholarship committees in regard to their financial situations, academic performance, career plans and extracurricular activities.

vi. All the students are notified of the outcomes by late June or early July.

Additional information regarding contacts and application process can be obtained from the Foundation's website:

http://www.akdn.org/our-agencies/aga-khan-foundation/international-scholarship-programme

## 5. OFID Scholarship Award for International Students

This award is offered to International students from developing countries who have demonstrated outstanding academic excellence and are pursuing a Masters" Degree study in any field that is relevant and development worthy. The studies can be undertaken in any of the accredited Universities worldwide. Areas of study for which the scholarship is offered may include; Masters" Degree in economics of development in fields related to energy and sustainable development, poverty reduction, environment and science and technology related fields. The award is open for citizens from developing countries.

**Scholarship Value**

The value of the scholarship is $50,000 and covers areas like tuition fees, monthly allowances for living expenses,

Insurance, books, accommodation, travel expenses and relocation grants.

**Eligibility**

- The applicant should be within the age limit of between 23 – 32 years at the time of application.
- The applicant is required to must have obtained an undergraduate degree with Baccalaureate from a University that is accredited or should be in the verge of accomplishing their undergraduate degree studies.
- Must have an admission letter to a University that is accredited and should be a full-time student in the University all through the duration of the Masters" degree.
- The applicant must be a citizen of a developing country and should have a subject selection that pertains to OFID's core missions.
- The deadline for that application is 1st of May.

More information can be accessed from the website: http://www.ofid.org/FOCUS-AREAS/Beyond-the-scope/Scholarship-Award

## 6. Joint Japan World Bank Graduate Scholarship Program

The Joint Japan World Bank Graduate Scholarship Program offers scholarship awards to students from developing countries who are pursuing Masters" program at the selected universities. The scholars are required to return to their countries after completion of the Masters" program to utilize the acquired knowledge and skills towards growth and development of their communities and countries. The scholarship is available to students from developing countries.

**Scholarship Value**

The scholarship is fully funded and the amount vary depending on the varied costs of tuition fees which is unique to every university.

The benefits include:

- Tuition fees for the graduate program
- Economy class air travel expenses
- Living expenses, basic medical insurance expenses

**Eligibility**

To be eligible for the award, the applicant should be able to meet the following requirements:

- Be a citizen of a country that is World Bank member. Some of the countries that are World Bank members include; Afghanistan, Algeria, Indonesia, India amongst others.
- The applicant should not be a dual citizen of any developed country
- The applicant should be below 45 years of age at the time of submitting the application.

- The applicant should be a holder of a Bachelor's degree or an equivalent University degree and should be one that dates before 2013.
- The applicant should have at least three years of experience in development related areas since earning the Bachelor's degree or within the past six years from the date of application deadline.
- Except for funding purposes, the applicant should have unconditional acceptance to enroll in the University in the upcoming academic year in one of the universities selected by the organization.
- The applicant is expected to be in good health and should have the capacity to be productive as a scholar and on full time basis over the duration of the Master's program. The applicant's health should be certified by a medical doctor three months before the starting off of the Master's program.

- The applicant should not be having another scholarship or support towards the Masters" program.
- The deadline for submitting applications is 10th March.

More information can be found at:

http://go.worldbank.org/H2H0TN2W10

## 7. Robert S. McNamara Research Fellowships

This program offers scholarship awards to applicants from developing countries who are pursuing PhD studies. The award is to enable them conduct doctoral research and development related and innovative research. The research should be conducted under the supervision of an advisor and should be with the host Institution for a period of between 6 to 10 months. The scholarship is available to students from developing countries whose country is a member of World Bank.

The studies can be carried in any preferred institution world over provided the below conditions are met:

**Scholarship Value**

The value of the scholarship is $25,000 and takes care of costs that are related to research program.

**Eligibility**

To be able to qualify for the scholarship, applicants are expected to meet the following requirements:

- You should be citizen of a country that is a World Bank member and should not be a dual citizen with a developed country that is not eligible for World Bank financing.
- The applicant is expected to have completed all the coursework and exams that is related to the PhD program by the date of the application deadline.
- The applicant should be at least be 35 years of age or below by the time of submitting the application.
- The applicant should not be an executive director, a staff member or have any appointment with the World Bank.
- The applicant should not be a previous recipient of the World Bank Robert S. McNamara Fellowships Program.

- The applicant should have their research proposal for the funding endorsed by the PhD thesis supervisor and the research advisor of the host institution
- The applicant should be able to demonstrate that they are able to complete their research program within a period of between 6-10 months.
- The deadline for the application is 2nd of February

To Apply: http://go.worldbank.org/993QOP76R0

## 8. The Dalai Lama Trust Graduate (MA and PhD)

The Dalai Lama is offering scholarship opportunities to students pursuing graduate programs in any of the accredited Universities in United States, Australia or Europe. The award is available to students from India or Nepal who are of Tibetan descent. The scholarship is awarded for the purpose of furthering human capital development amongst the Tibetan people and also towards enhancing pursuit of excellence in the fields of graduate studies.

The scholarship is provided for pursuing Masters" Degree programs and PhD and is awarded to the selected applicants in the field of choice.

## Scholarship Value

The value of the scholarship is $10,000 and is only given to students who have demonstrated academic excellence in their chosen fields of study.

## Eligibility

To be eligible for the scholarship, the applicant should be able to meet the below requirements:

- Must be enrolled in any accredited Universities from the stated countries for a full time graduate degree program.
- The applicant should be able to show proof of Tibetan heritage.

- The applicant should be pursuing graduate studies either at a Masters' level, PhD be in a Law School or a Professional School.
- Applicants will be required to demonstrate proof of proficiency in English language

To Apply: http://www.dalailamatrust.org/scholarship

## 9. Asian Development Bank/Japan Scholarship Program.

This program is offering scholarship awards to scholars who are pursuing postgraduate studies in economics, science and technology and management faculties. The applicants are selected depending on merit and demonstrated excellence in areas of study. The studies can be carried out at the accredited universities in the United States, Australia and other countries mentioned in the website.

**Scholarship Value**

The award takes care of full tuition fees, housing expenses, a monthly allowance for living expenses, instructional materials, books travel expenses, medical insurance cover. Scholars that are involved in research will be able to receive a special grant that can be used for thesis preparation. In some cases, the scholarship may also cover preparatory language, computer literacy and other related expenses.

**Eligibility**

- To be eligible for the award, the applicant should be at least 35 years or below by the time of submitting the application. The applicant should also be in good health and should have a bachelor's degree or its equivalent by the time of submitting the application.
- The scholars should be able to return to their countries of origin once the studies are completed to contribute to their nation's social and economic development.

- The scholarships are open to students from countries like Cambodia, Mongolia, Papua New Guinea, Indonesia, India, Tajikistan amongst others.

Applications should be submitted in six months before the date of admission to college.

To Apply: https://www.adb.org/site/careers/japan-scholarship-program/procedures-applying

## 10. Rotary Foundation Global Scholarship Grants for Development

Rotary Foundation provides awards to students undertaking graduate level degrees and Research for a period of either four years or two years. The scholarship is focused to address six areas; Peace and conflict resolution, Prevention of disease and treatment, water and sanitation, Maternal and child health, economic and community development and basic education and literacy. The award is given to students who are not members of Rotary Club.

## Scholarship Value

The minimum value of the award is $30,000 and takes care of Passport and visa expenses, travel expenses, Tuition fees, living expenses, school supplies. The award can also take care of language training expenses but that only happens if language proficiency requirement is met as per the given admission.

## Eligibility

To be eligible for the training, the applicant should meet the following requirements:

- The applicant should not be a Rotarian or an employee of a club or district or any other Rotary entity or neither a spouse or close relative.
- The applicant is required to study outside their home country and should be able to provide proof of University admission by the time of submitting the application letters. Conditional admission is allowed in situations

where the Institution require financial guarantee or completion of undergraduate degree.

- The applicant should demonstrate proof of being involved in some previous work or volunteer activities and academic reports. The applicant's career plans should be at least aligned to one of the six areas that the Rotary Foundation is focused on.
- Interested applicants can visit any of the local Rotary clubs for more information. The application forms can also be accessed online and be filled accordingly.
- The applications can be submitted all through the year however the applicant should try and submit the application three months before the beginning of academic year.

More information regarding the grant can be accessed from the website: https://www.rotary.org/myrotary/en/take-action/apply-grants/global-grants

## 11. Fulbright Foreign Student Program in USA

Fulbright Nehru awards provides students that have demonstrated outstanding academic excellence with the opportunity to study in the United States. This program provides graduate students, artists and young professionals with the opportunity to pursue their studies and conduct research from the United States Universities. The applicants from diverse fields including interdisciplinary ones can apply. The award is available to International students from around 155 countries all over the world. Some of the countries include: Nepal, Tajikistan, India, Egypt, Morocco, Bahrain amongst others.

The selection process for Indian students is generally rigorous and once the students have qualified they get support that enables them to navigate through the visa process, comprehensive pre-departure orientation including securing of health insurance.

**Scholarship Value**

The award takes care of full tuition fees, travel expenses, health insurance, living expenses and the award is available for the entire period of study. The award amount may vary depending on the choice of University.

**Eligibility**

The eligibility requirements differ depending on the country from which one is applying from: Indian citizens can apply for either student awards which enables them to study in the US or conduct research, they can also apply for scholars and teachers awards which enables them to either teach or carry out research. Applicants also get awards for professional development programs which enable them to develop leadership and specialized skills that enables them to effectively serve as University administrators.

- The selection team identifies applicants with projects that are relevant to India and the United States.

- Applicants should be able to demonstrate the potential to be effective cultural ambassadors.
- The information regarding the scholarship can be accessed from USIEF offices that are in New Delhi, Chennai, Kolkata, Hyderabad and Mumbai.

The deadline for submitting the applications is 31st of December.

More information can be accessed at:

http://www.usief.org.in/index.aspx

## 12. Hubert Humphrey Fellowships in USA for International Students

This scholarship is for professionals that are interested in enhancing their leadership skills through exchange of knowledge and understanding of issues with common concern. The scholarship is for a non-degree program and can be undertaken in any of the selected universities within the United States depending on their area of study. Some of the fields of study include; Agricultural and Rural development, economic development, Public Health Policy and Management amongst others.

The scholarship is available to citizens for students from the following regions: Middle East and North Africa, Sub-Saharan Africa, South and Central Asia amongst others.

## Scholarship Value

The scholarship takes care of full funding with tuition fees paid directly to the host University. The award may also cater for English language training if necessary.

The award takes care of maintenance and living expenses, a one-time settling in allowance, health insurance and accident cover, books allowance, one-time computer subsidy, Air Travel to and from the United States, professional development allowance that takes care of field trips, conferences and professional visits.

## Eligibility

- To be eligible for the program, the applicant should have an undergraduate degree with a minimum of five years of full-time work experience.
- The applicant should have very limited or no experience in the United States.
- The applicant should demonstrate proficiency in English language and be able to show proven leadership qualities with a record showing engagement in community services.
- The deadline for submitting the applications is 30th of September.

More information about the scholarship can be accessed at:

https://www.humphreyfellowship.org

## 13. Stanford Reliance Dhirubhai Fellowship

Stanford Reliance Dhirubhai Fellowship was created by Reliance Industries Limited with the sole purpose of providing financial support to Indian nations who are in need of financial support towards pursuing MBA programs at Stanford University.

Stanford GSB has demonstrated great emphasis towards Global Management Education and Institution is quite proud of having enrolled many Indian Nationals through the years. The foundation hopes that Indian men and women who have demonstrated excellent academic achievement and are equally talented but lack the financial aid that can enable them enroll in the business school get encouraged to apply for the scholarship.

The students are provided with quality educational foundation that may enable them to effect positive change in India. The beneficiaries are however expected to return to India and get to lead organizations that are at the forefront of steering the country towards growth and development.

**Scholarship Value**

The fellowship provides financial support that takes care of the tuition fees and other related expenses. The value of the scholarship is approximately $150,000 per year for a period of two years.

## Eligibility

To be considered eligible for the program, applicants are expected to meet the following requirements:

Must meet all the requirements by the Stanford application requirements which include proof of proficiency in English language by providing certificates for IELTS, PTE, TOEFL, academic transcripts amongst others.

Applicants should be able to demonstrate intellectual vitality, leadership potential, outstanding personal qualities and contributions.

Selection is done in reference to one's commitment to develop India, merit and the level of financial need.

Application for the scholarship is done online through the Fellowship's website. Applicants are expected to submit Graduate Management Admission Test (GMAT) OR Graduate record examination if available.

Official transcripts should not be submitted alongside the application letter instead the submission should be done later when the applicant gets invited for an interview.

Letter of recommendations should also be submitted later after the applicant is considered for interviewing. Finalists will be required to submit two letters of recommendation for their MBA application.

A 250 word essay should be submitted with the application letter including the applicant's financial information.

The deadline for submitting the application is 15th of June. Finalists will get notified by the 7th of July.

More information can be accessed from the website: https://www.gsb.stanford.edu/programs/mba/financial-aid/international-students/stanford-reliance-dhirubhai-fellowship

## 14.ICSP Scholarships at University of Oregon USA

The award is available to University students who have demonstrated exceptional merit and financial need and are interested in pursuing faculties with a cultural component at the University of Oregon. ICSP Scholarship has a cultural component and students are required to deliver presentations regarding their home countries to community organization, children, University of Oregon students, staff and faculty.

**Scholarship Value**

The value of the scholarship may range from $7,500 to $30,000

**Eligibility**

The following requirements should be met by the applicants if they are to be considered for the award:

- Applicants are expected to meet all the admission requirements before applying for the award and new students should apply for admission to the University.

- Applicants should not be United States citizens, permanent residents or should not be eligible to receive federal financial assistance.
- Applicants should demonstrate requirement of financial assistance and should be able to meet the 3.0 cumulative GPA requirement.
- The students should commit to completing 80 hours of cultural service per year as required by the program.
- Applicants are required to complete the application form alongside supporting documents.
- The deadline for submitting application forms is 15th January

More information can be accessed at: http://uoregon.edu/apply

## 15. International Peace Scholarships for Women

The international peace scholarship fund is provided to women from other countries giving them opportunity to study in the US and Canada. The members believe that quality education is fundamental for a world of peace and understanding. The scholarship is given as per demonstrated need and may not cover all the academic and personal expenses.

The maximum scholarship amount that can be awarded is $12,500 with lesser amounts awarded as per the individual's need.

**Eligibility**

i. The applicant must be qualified for full time enrollment as a graduate student working towards a graduate degree in an accredited university within the United States or Canada.

ii. To qualify for the first scholarship, the applicant must be having a full year of course work remaining and is enrolled and in residence for the entire college year.

iii. Doctoral students who have completed coursework and working on dissertations need not eligible to apply.

iv. Consideration for admission is based on academic performance, provision of ACT and SAT scores, provision of academic recommendations that demonstrated potential for academic success.

    iv. Application forms can be accessed at the programs website: http://www.peointernational.org

## 16. Microsoft's Research Women's Fellowship Program

The Microsoft Research Women's Fellowship is committed to providing funding to women who are interested in pursuing PhD courses and the study is limited to a selected list of academic Universities within the United States. The award is available to international women students pursuing PhD studies. And the course is offered at any level in any of the following selected Universities amongst others:

i. Carnegie Mellon University

ii. Princeton University

iii. University of Texas at Austin

iv. University of Washington.

**Scholarship Value**

The Scholarship awarded is a total of $20,000 and $18,000 covers tuition fees and $2,000 covers travel expenses to conferences related to field of study.

**Eligibility**

i. The scholarship award is only available for one academic year and will not be extended or renewed.

ii. Only women applicants who are either entering or already enrolled for PhD in any of the selected Universities are eligible for the award.

iii. The recipient is expected to be actively engaged as full time students during their PhD level studies at any of the Universities and failure to do that may result in termination of the award.

iv. Opportunities will be made for the successful applicants to engage with researchers from Microsoft in their diverse study domains as well as collaboration in community work.

v. Information regarding how to apply and requirements can be obtained at: https://www.microsoft.com/en-us/research/academic-program/womens-fellowship-program/

## 17. Clark Global Scholarship Program

Clark Global Scholarship Program is based on the University's commitment to providing education that is globally focused and challenging. Clark University awards international students with scholarship based on merit. The program is hosted by Clark University in Massachusetts, USA and eligible for International students taking Bachelor's degree offered at the University.

**Value of Scholarship**

Below are some of the details of what one gets access to if they are considered for the award:

i. You will receive a scholarship amount of between $5,000 - $25,000 per year and renewal will be subject to meeting the required academic standards

ii. You will receive $2,500 guaranteed taxable allowance for paid internship or research assistantship that is carried out during summer for academic credit during junior or sophomore period.

iii. You will get a chance to participate in the global scholars' mentor program which also includes an annual buffet dinner that is normally hosted by the president of Clark University.

iv. You will get an opportunity for guidance by alumni leadership mentors or the staff and you will also be assigned to a faculty advisor for closer attention.

**Eligibility**

To be eligible for the scholarship, you must have the following:

i. You must be a first-year applicant and not a student transferring from another college or university and must have attended school overseas for a period of over four years.

ii. International citizens that are attending school in the US will are also eligible to apply for the scholarship.

iii. The student should be able to demonstrate the potential of providing leadership both in the community and world over and should also be committed to making a difference at both levels.

To Apply: http://www.clarku.edu/scholarships-first-year-international-students#global

i. The students that are eligible should be able to apply before 15 January (this deadline is for 2017, and varies by year).

ii. Application forms and other details can be accessed at the University's website.

iii. The official scholarship website is http://www.clarku.edu/scholarships-first-year-international-students#global

### 18. Berea College

This is one of the colleges in the United States that provide 100% funding to all the 100% enrolled International students. The students are eligible for undertaking Bachelor of Arts and Bachelor of Science in 28 fields. The Scholarship amounts cover costs of tuition, boarding, room charges and fees. In the previous years, International Students were expected to save at least $1000 per year to use towards their expenses and the college provides summer jobs that can enable the international students meet the obligation.

Once the international students are accepted for enrollment, they are expected to pay an entrance fee of $50 and a deposit of

$2,200 as a confirmation for the enrollment. The deposit can then be utilized by the International students within the period of four years for their expenses. Additional aid can still be given to students who are unable to pay the deposit either partially or full amount.

All the International students are given paid jobs within the campus through the college's work program that runs all through the academic year. Students can then use their wages which can be around $1,800 in the first year to take care of their personal expenses.

**Eligibility**

Students of all nationalities, religious faiths, races and ethnicities are eligible to apply for the scholarship. However, the admission process is quite competitive with specific criteria required to be met for consideration.

The deadline for International application ends on 30 November

## Scholarship Amount

The full tuition scholarship amount is equivalent to $100,000 for a period of four years.

To apply: https://www.berea.edu/admissions/applying-for-admission/international-students/application/

i. You can complete the Berea College Application for admission and Scholarship form. The form is available online and there is no fee required for the application.

ii. Once you have filled the form, you can schedule an appointment for your interview.

iii. You should also be able to get filled and submitted evaluation and endorsement forms. The forms should be filled by a current or former teacher, principal, community leader or school administrator.

iv. Fill guidance and counselor Evaluation form

v. Financial Eligibility requirement to be appropriately filled.

vi. Official High School Transcript

vii. Official CAT or SAT scores.

viii. International Personal Essay with essay cover sheet.

ix. Personal statement and resume is optional but is encouraged for better understanding. Name and date of birth should be included in all the pages of the Application form.

x. All the completed applications forms alongside other components must be mailed as a batch. The batch to include high school records, test scores and recommendations and International students are not allowed to apply online.

The official scholarship website is

https://www.berea.edu/admissions/applying-for-admission

## 19. East-West Centre Graduate Degree Fellowship

East-West Centre provides scholarships to students from Asia, the Pacific and United States that are pursuing graduate study at the University of Hawaii. The graduates eligible should be undertaking Masters' and doctoral studies and should be willing to take part in educational, residential community building, cultural and leadership development programs at the University of Hawaii. The main purpose of East – West Centre is to effectively impact Asia-Pacific community by equipping the students for future leadership roles.

The scholarship covers the following areas:

i. Full time graduate fees and tuition cost equivalent to the tuition charged, books and housing in an East-West Center residence hall based on single occupancy.

ii. A stipend to partially cover expenses for meals and incidental expenses.

iii. Funding for field study alongside conference presentation is offered during the period of study on a competitive basis.

iv. Subsidy towards health insurance coverage.

v. Students with commitment to Asia-Pacific will be given priority.

vi. The grants are initially made for twelve months but are subject to renewal depending on funds availability.

vii. Degree applicants who are not residents of the USA are required to come on the program through Exchange visitor (J-1) visa and are also subject to all the requirements to the provisions of the Exchange Visa Program. For more information about the Visa you can get in touch through: wongv@eastwestcenter.org

**Scholarship Approval Details for Indian Students:**

EWC housing award - $420 per month

Living Expense - $600 per month

EWS Program Fees - $7,000

**Eligibility**

To be considered for enrollment, those applying for the graduate programs are required to have obtained a 4-year bachelor's degree from one of the recognized universities within the US or from an equivalent recognized college or university abroad. The applicant is required to have a minimum grade of 3.0 point on the average or an equivalent in all the previous four semesters. He may also have scored the same in the last six quarters of his/her undergraduate record and in all his/her baccalaureate.

The East-West Centre graduate degree fellowships are meant to support graduate study at the University of Hawaii in areas and fields that are in line with the goals and objectives of the centre including advanced degree at the University of Hawaii. To be enrolled for study at the University of Hawaii, you have to first apply to the East-West Centre. Application to the university and to the centre can be submitted concurrently alongside all supporting documents to the East-West Centre.

The deadline for submitting the applications is November 1 for the study to begin the following August.

The application forms can be downloaded from the university's website. The forms to be downloaded include:

i. Application guide

ii. Application checklist

iii. Application form and instructions

iv. Essay questions and instructions

v. Academic letter of reference form and instructions

vi. Civic engagement letter of reference form and instructions

vii. Verification of funds for additional expenses form

viii. GDF application forms

In case you are unable to download the forms then you can request for the forms through this email:

scholarships@eastwestcentre.org

For the University of Hawaii graduate degree application documents, you can access the application documents from the university's website here:

https://manoa.hawaii.edu/graduate/content/graduate-programs

The application forms include:

i. UHM notice to applicants

ii. Admissions forms and application instructions for the graduates

iii. Graduate admission application forms

iv. Statement of objectives form.

v. Download departmental application forms in regard to the academic program you are applying for.

Program specific application forms can be accessed at:
http://www.manoa.hawaii.edu/graduate/content/grad

# List of Scholarships for Studying in UK and Europe

Though tuition at European universities is a lot more affordable than US, there are several universities in both the UK and other EU countries that are still not affordable to most people in India.

## 1. Goa Education Trust Scholarships

The Goa education trust was started with the main aim of providing Goan students with an opportunity to undertake higher education degrees and post graduate studies in the UK. The scholarship is however also open to Indian nationals that are interested in pursuing Master's program in the UK.

**Eligibility**

The following requirements should be met by the applicant in order to be considered for the award:

- The applicant should be able to identify the Master's program that they find suitable and application be done by the beginning of September.
- The applicant should be an Indian National with a valid Passport and must be living in India at the time of applying for the Scholarship.
- The applicant should not be more than 30 years of age by the time of applying for the scholarship.
- The applicant should have an excellent academic records and achievements in extra-curricular activities.

**Scholarship Value**

The value of the scholarship is £12,500 which is anticipated to cover in part or full tuition expenses

- The application forms can be accessed online from the website.

- Once the form has been downloaded, it should be filled in word format with the applicant's photo fixed in the appropriate place.
- The following documents should also be scanned and sent alongside the application form
    - Copy of the Applicant's birth certificate for proof of age
    - Copy of passport details with proof of applicant's address.
    - Copy of admission letter to the UK institution if already received.
    - One professional and academic recommendation letter with recent graduates submitting two academic reference letters.
- The entire package of application documents including the scanned copies of academic transcripts, motivation letter and form with photograph should all be emailed to: get.scholarship@britishcouncil.org

- In case the applicant is unable to submit the application electronically then the same set of documents should be emailed to the address provided in the Institutions website.

The deadline for submitting application forms is the 15th of May.

More information can be obtained from the institutions website: https://www.scholarshipsinindia.com/goa-education-trust-GET-scholarships.html

## 2. GREAT Scholarships India

These scholarships are provided to over 500000 students in over 200 countries who wish to study in the UK, including India. For the year 2017, there are 48 different scholarships in partnership with 40 universities in the UK.

**Scholarship Amount**

The scholarship amounts differ between 5000 – 10000 pounds, depending on the award and the university.

## 3. Emile Boutmy Scholarships for Non-EU Students at Sciences PO

The scholarships program was created with the sole aim of attracting excellent International students from various parts of the world and outside the European Union. The Science Po started the Emile Boutmy Scholarship and is one of the best University's in France that works in collaboration with four other Parisian Universities and offers higher education and high quality research.

The quality of research covers a worldwide perspective in all disciplines and gives international students an opportunity to enhance their training and research capabilities to an international scale as they choose Masters' students of a high caliber.

**Eligibility**

- To be eligible for Emile Boutmy Scholarship, the applicant should be applying for the first time and should be coming

- from a non-European state with a household that does not file for taxes within the European Union.
- The scholarship is available for students who have been admitted for undergraduate or Master programs that are offered at the University.
- Applicants with dual citizenship that includes European Union States are eligible for the scholarship.
- The Emile Boutmy Scholarship cannot be supplemented with other scholarships like the Eiffel scholarship, AEFE scholarship and others. The award is also available to exchange students.
- Applicants with dual degree on areas like Journalism sciences and dual degree in sciences are also eligible for the scholarship.

## Scholarship Value

The value of the scholarship awarded by Emile Boutmy program takes diverse forms like:

For undergraduate students, an award of € 7,300 per year is awarded for a period of three years with an additional grant of €5,000 to take care of the cost of living. A grant amount of €3,000 - €7,300 can also be awarded for the undergraduate students minus the grant that can take care of the cost of living. In exceptional circumstances a scholarship amount of € 19,000 can also be granted to the undergraduate students for a period of three years.

If you get awarded the scholarship and then decide to defer it then it will automatically be lost. If you fail to validate your academic year then your scholarship can also be lost.

For the Masters' level students, an award of € 10,000 is given to take care of tuition fees for the period of two years and € 6,000 is also given to cover cost of living per year. Others may get an award of around € 5,000 - € 10, 000 to take care of tuition fees. A scholarship amount of € 19,000 can also be awarded per year in situations that are exceptional.

The deadline for submitting applications for undergraduate programs is 2nd of May.

The deadline for Masters" Program is 13th of January

The process of application can be accessed online through the Institution's website.

Ensure that you have all the necessary documents required for application in an electronic format. The application form should be downloaded and filled accordingly and the documents to be uploaded should also be scanned and sent alongside the application form. It is not possible to send the documents through post and all the documents are to be submitted electronically.

There is a list of all the required documents on the Institution website and you can get the details once you begin the registration process. Once you have submitted your application form and the required documents, you can then track the process of your application through the online Science PO student's page.

You can update your file if at all it is not complete by following the instructions given in the administration tab.

More information can be accessed from the Institution's website: http://formation.sciences-po.fr/en/contenu/the-emile-boutmy-scholarship

## 4. ESED Scholarship for Sustainable Energy Development Studies

ESED Scholarship is focused towards supporting outstanding students who are pursuing Master's degree studies in sustainable energy development and is geared towards encouraging meaningful contributions in the relevant areas. The focus group for the award are international students from developing countries and studies can be undertaken from any accredited University in the world.

**Scholarship Value**

The value of the scholarship is $23,000 per year and is awarded for the Masters' studies level for two years.

**Eligibility**

To be considered for the award, the applicant should be able to meet the following requirements:

- The applicant should be able to undertake studies in areas that are related to sustainable energy development.
- The applicant should be a national of developing countries and should be amongst the top 20% from their class with excellent academic results alongside a history of involvement in community activities.
- The applicant should express determination towards advancing in their knowledge and understanding and should be willing to undertake studies in areas sustainable energy development
- The applicant should be ready to return back to their home country after completion of the Masters" program.

- The deadline of the scholarship is 4th March

More information can be accessed from the website:

https://scholarship.globalelectricity.org/account/sign-in

## 5. Marshall Papworth Scholarships for Agriculture

Marshal Papworth Scholarship for Agriculture is an award offered to students who are pursuing Masters" studies in subjects related to Agriculture and horticulture development areas and runs for a period of one year. The studies are undertaken at the accredited Universities within the UK and the award is available to students from developing countries.

**Scholarship Amount**

The value of the scholarship of the scholarship may vary depending on the location of the chosen University. The value of the scholarship may range from £14,500 to £21,500. The award takes care of living expenses, tuition fees and travel expenses.

**Eligibility**

- Applicants cannot apply directly to the Marshal Papworth Fund and should instead select their choice of university from amongst the chosen ones then apply for their desired course.
- The applicant is expected to have a good command of English language as they will be required to sit for English tests.
- Once the applications are submitted to the Universities, selection will then be done by the Universities and the candidate that is found to be eligible for the course will have their application and CV forwarded to Marshal Papworth Scholarship for further consideration.
- The selected applicants should be able to demonstrate a strong desire to impact their country and people with the knowledge gained.
- Applicants who will be considered for the award will not have received any form of funding prior to submitting the application.

- The deadline for submitting the applications is 14th of April.

More information can be accessed at:

http://www.marshalpapworth.com/how-to-apply/how-to-apply-for-the-Masters'-programme/

## 6. Charles Wallace India Trust Awards

This award is focused towards providing mid-career students with an opportunity to pursue their studies in the UK and get to gain a wider experience and exposure. The duration of the award may range from 3 months to one year and the program does not support a two year program. The areas of study should be covering performance, visual arts, photography, film, design, art history, curating including conservation architecture and management of heritage sites or projects.

**Scholarship Value**

The value of the scholarship vary depending on the selected institution but it covers accommodation and living costs, tuition fees and travelling expenses.

**Eligibility**

- The applicant must be an Indian citizen that is living in India and should be aged between 25 and 38 years by the time of submitting the application form.
- The applicant must have obtained a first degree, diploma or any professional qualification in the fields relevant to their studies.
- The applicant should not have received a CWIT grant in a period of 5 years before the time of submitting the application.
- The application forms should be filled and submitted at the British Council Centre as hard copies. The application should include a statement of purpose which is not more than two pages and should clearly outline the course you

intend to take, what you intend to engage in while in the UK and your action plan on how you will put the information into use once you return back to India.

- The applicant will also provide evidence of unconditional acceptance to the chosen University or college, evidence of progress towards acceptance, any internship if you have applied for such and attachment of IELTS certificate for proof of language proficiency.

- Although the British Council facilitates the process and offers advice as desired, the cost of the visa should be taken care of by the applicant.

- The deadline for submitting the scholarship is 30$^{th}$ November.

More information can be accessed at:

https://www.britishcouncil.in/study-uk/scholarships/charles-wallace-trust/long-term

7. **TRACE International Scholarship**

This award is offered to exceptionally young leaders from the developing countries like Asia, Africa, Middle East amongst others with the aim of increasing transparency while at the same time reducing corruption. The applicants should demonstrate interest in pursuing an LLM with the focus of advancing commercial transparency and raising of anti-bribery compliance standards all over the world. The applicants are expected to demonstrate an interest in criminal law and anti-corruption efforts. The applicant should therefore be able to enroll in courses that are relevant like International law, Criminal law, governance and economic development and rule of law. The scholarship can be taken at a University within the UK.

**Scholarship Value**

The organization provides full funding that caters for tuition fee, accommodation and living expenses, travel expenses and may also include Visa processing expenses.

**Eligibility**

- The applicant should have a first degree in law or its equivalent and should be a citizen of a developing country as defined by the World Bank.
- The applicant should be willing to return to their home country after completion of the studies.
- Applicants are required to meet specific English language requirements with strong demonstration of English language. The scores should be equivalent to 580 for TOEFL and 92 for TOEFLiBT.
- The applicant should demonstrate leadership skills and should be willing to take interviews through Skype.
- A completed application form alongside the relevant documents should then be forwarded to the Graduate Tutor at Kings College.
- The deadline for submitting the application form is 7th of January.

More information can be accessed at:

http://www.buddy4study.com/scholarship/trace-international-scholarship-2017-18

## 9. The Rhodes Trust

The Rhodes Trust provides awards to postgraduate students that have demonstrated outstanding and all round achievement and are willing to pursue their studies at the University of Oxford. The scholarship is provided in partnership with John McCall McBain who is the second century founder alongside others. The award is offered to citizens of countries like Hong Kong, India, South Africa, United Arab Emirates, Zambia, Zimbabwe amongst others.

The Rhodes Trust is focused in four areas which influences the criteria used in the selection process:

- Scholastic and literary attainments
- Demonstration of exemplary achievements in areas such as sports, artistic pursuits and areas where teamwork is

involved. The applicant should show the ability to use their energy to the fullest.

- Demonstration of truth, courage, fellowship, unselfishness, protection of the weak amongst others.
- Demonstration of moral force of character and having the instincts to lead and showing of interest in other fellow beings.

In summary Rhodes Scholarship selection team is interested in supporting young men and women that have demonstrated outstanding intellect, leadership, character and commitment to service.

## Scholarship Value

The scholarship covers all the University and college fees. It also takes care of a personal stipend, one economy class airfare, and economy flight back to the Scholars home country after completion of the studies.

## Eligibility

To be eligible for the scholarship; the following requirements should be met by the applicant

- The applicant should be holding their first degree and the students should be getting an award for a two year study period which can also be extended to three years.
- The applicant should have first class scores in all the relevant disciplines.
- The applicant should be aged between 19 and 25 or 27 for those pursuing medical or doctoral courses.
- Applicants are required to provide birth certificates as proof of their age and certified copies of their degrees and other academic results.
- Applicants should provide information regarding any employment they had engaged in or any business undertaking they were involved with after completion of their first degree programs.

- Applicants should provide a detailed CV including proof of involvement in other extracurricular activities like sports, cultural and community activities.
- Applicants should include a personal statement of about 1000 words indicating their future career plans once the studies are completed, express priorities and aims they are intending to make in the society, express chosen field of study and demonstrate that they are capable of meeting the requirements of the chosen field.
- The applicant should write the statement on their own and sign it without seeking for any person's help.
- The people listed as referees should have valid working contacts with details on how they can be contacted
- Proof of English language proficiency should be provided by students who English is not their first language.
- Each applicant should be able to fulfill citizenry and residency requirements.

- The deadline for submitting the application is 15$^{th}$ of August

More Information can be accessed at:

http://www.rhodeshouse.ox.ac.uk/apply

## 10. Lle De France Master Scholarship

The lle-De-France scholarship is available to students who intend to pursue Masters" Degree in Paris. The scholarship is awarded for a period of one year and is renewable upon submission of application. The scholarship form should be filled and sent to the respective University or college and it is the institution that then applies on behalf of the student. Students are not allowed to send their applications directly to the Regional Council.

## Scholarship Value

The value of the scholarship is €10,500, accommodation is reserved for the students at Cite Universitaire in Paris.

## Eligibility

- The applicant should be less than 30 years of age
- The applicant should not be in France at the time of submitting the application
- The applicant should not be a bi-national; for example, Indian-French.
- The applicant should be committed to pursuing a Masters" degree program in the lle-De-France region for a period that is not less than 10 consecutive months.
- The applicant should not be having any other scholarship from the French government or from the region.

The deadline for the application is: 31st March.

More information can be accessed at: https://www.iledefrance.fr

## 11. Dr. Manmohan Singh Scholarships

This scholarship is aimed at supporting students from India who are interested in pursuing doctoral studies at St. John's College, Cambridge. The selected students are expected to gain knowledge that will enable them to become leading achievers and be of great value to the Indian society. Applicants are required to first submit applications to the University of Cambridge with selection to St. John College as their first choice.

**Scholarship Value**

The scholarship will take care of the following:

- Tuition fees
- International Airfare
- Monthly allowance that takes care of living expenses
- UK visa charges.

**Eligibility**

To be considered eligible for the award, applicants should be able to meet the following requirements:

- The applicant should be an Indian citizen with a valid Indian Passport and should be residing in India at the time of submitting the application.

- The applicant should be below 35 years of age at the time of submitting the application form.
- The applicant should not be receiving any funding from the UK or any significant exposure to the UK education.
- The applicant should be a holder of a Masters" degree from a reputable University in India and should have a first class award in the relevant field of study.
- The applicant should have the intention of pursuing a full time doctoral research degree from the University of Cambridge.
- The applicant should be ready to demonstrate leadership qualities including extracurricular activities, community work or any contribution made to the society.
- The applicant should demonstrate proof of proficiency in English language and should be able to fulfill all the academic criteria as required by the University.

- Applications should ensure that they go through the application guidelines and be able to fill the application forms accordingly

- The application forms can be accessed online and the deadline for submitting the application is 15$^{th}$ of January.

More information can be accessed from the website: http://www.joh.cam.ac.uk/dr-manmohan-singh-scholarships

## 12. Amsterdam Excellence Scholarships

Amsterdam's Excellence scholarships are offered to students from outside Europe who have demonstrated exceptional talents and academic excellence and are pursuing Master's programs that are offered at the University of Amsterdam. The application is allowed for non-EU citizens who have demonstrated academic excellence, ambition and have shown relevance in the selected Master's program study area.

The Masters" program should be running for two years and there are options for extension of scholarship for a second year. The recipients also form part of a select committee and are expected to participate in programs developed for them like the extracurricular activities amongst others.

**Eligibility**

- To be eligible for the scholarship, the applicant must have graduated at the top of their classes and be among the leading 10%. The Master's studies can be undertaken in the following areas:

i) Amsterdam Law School

ii) Faculty of science

iii) Graduate School of Humanities

iv) Graduate School of Social Sciences

v) Faculty of Economics and Business

- The applicants should not be eligible for study grants or support under the Dutch system and in case of any change in Nationality, the residential permit or even a possible support, the scholarship office should be immediately notified of any change at any time all through the academic year.

- The applicant should be for the first time applying for admission at the University of Amsterdam for a Masters" program as students seeking second Masters" degree are not eligible for the award.
- The applicant should be able to comply with the visa regulations as required by the Dutch Immigration Service.
- The applicant should be enrolled as a fulltime student at the University of Amsterdam for the period in which the Scholarship is awarded. The award is not guaranteed in case of any change to another Master's program.
- The applicant should not be in receipt of another scholarship during the same period of study at the University of Amsterdam.
- The selection criteria are based on academic excellence and a promise to do better as demonstrated in the academic results.

- To apply for the scholarships, applicants should submit forms of application to the admission offices of the specific graduate schools.
- The applicant should demonstrate the educational quality of the previous institute where the previous graduate or undergraduate programs were taken.
- The applicant should obtain a letter of recommendation from the academic adviser, the dean, teacher or any other authority from the previous institution.
- The applicant should write a letter of motivation stating reasons why they chose the specific Master's program and elaborate into a broader context the relevance of the program towards their future career.
- The applicant should state various extracurricular activities that they can engage in like participation in student's commissions, music, sports, international experience or volunteer work.

- Provide proof of proficiency in English language with overall results from exams like IELTS, TOEFLS demonstrating a high of 100 and a minimum score of 22 in all of the components of the tests.
- The quality of the application form will also be examined in terms of accuracy of information, consistency and completeness.
- The application form should be printed and completed accordingly and the form should be submitted alongside letter of motivation, copy of university grade transcripts, certified copy of University Diploma, proof of English proficiency, two copies of letters of recommendation, description of extracurricular activities and the applicant's curriculum vitae.

## Scholarship Value

The Amsterdam Excellence Scholarship offers awards that cover tuition and living expenses for one academic year however there is possibility of the scholarship being extended for another year of the Master's program. The institution offers scholarship with the value being €25,000.

The deadline for the application is 1st February and more information can be accessed from the Institution's website:

http://www.uva.nl/en/education/master-s/scholarships--tuition/scholarships--tuition.html

## 13. Chevening UK Scholarships for International Students

Chevening is an International Scholarship scheme organized by the UK government with a focus geared towards developing global leaders. The funding is done by the Foreign and Commonwealth office and other partner organizations. Chevening provides two different kinds of awards and the selection is carried out through the British High Commission offices and Embassies all around the world.

The organization provides awards to prospective future leaders, decision makers and influencers all over the world with the opportunity to develop both academically and professionally and be able to experience the UK culture as they get to extensively network and build strong and lasting relationships with the UK.

The scholarship is open to students with leadership potential and are looking forward to studying a master's degree in any of the courses within the UK. The scholarship covers university tuition fees, travel costs, a monthly stipend, Visa application costs and travel grants for attending Chevening events within the UK.

**Scholarship Summary Package**

The award is to cover the following areas:

- University tuition fees payment
- Travel costs from the country of residence and back through an approved route and allowance on return back to country of residence.
- A grant is given if required towards preparation of dissertation or thesis.
- Allowance for excess baggage and visa cost for one person.

- A monthly stipend to take care of personal allowance, living expenses and accommodation. The stipend will be given with consideration to whether one is studying within London or outside. The allowance stands at £917 for those residing outside London and £1134 for those residing within London. The amount is however reviewed annually.
- The award amount for tuition fee is £14,500 but is subject to annual review.

**Eligibility**

In order to qualify for the scholarship, the applicant is required to fulfill the following:

- Should demonstrate proficiency in English by attaining the minimum requirement for English language at the time of remitting the application form.
- Should be a citizen of any of the countries that is eligible for Chevening award and should be willing to return to the country once the study period is completed. Applicants

from the following are eligible for the award; Asian countries like India, African countries, Middle East amongst others.

- Should be a holder of a degree that is equivalent to a good second class honors degree in the UK.
- Should have at least two years' work experience before the time of application.
- There is no age limit for the applicants if the above requirements are met.
- Application to Chevening can only be done through the online application system and you can begin by registering for Chevening Scholarship programs and then signing up through your Country's Chevening website for updates and notifications regarding the opening and closing dates.
- Once you are registered you will get notification on when to apply then you can complete an online eChevening application form. The opening and closing dates for applications will be available on the website.

- While filling the eChevening application form, you will be asked to demonstrate if you meet the required minimum proficiency in English language alongside academic details for Pierson PTE Academic, IELTS, and TOEFL including the scores received and certificate number.
- You will also include in the application form three UK universities that you may prefer attending in order of preference including the courses you intend to take. Apart from the eChevening application form, you should also apply separately to your preferred University.
- Once the applications are received they will be reviewed by a committee that is chaired by the Regional Adviser and Chevening's Scholarship Secretariat. The Regional Advisor will then make recommendations to the British High Commission or British Embassy regarding the candidates that can be invited for interview.
- The local British Embassy will then decide on the candidates to invite for interview and no reimbursement

on traveling expenses will be made to those invited for interview unless clearly stated in the application letter.
- It is advisable that you take time to read the application guidance before filling and submitting the application form.
- The closing date for the applications is 8th November.

You can get more information from the website:

http://www.chevening.org

## 14. Leiden University Excellence Scholarships

Application for scholarships from Leiden University is available for students from all nationalities who are pursuing studies in a master's degree program or those enrolling in Masters' of law advanced program or Masters' in International Relations and Diplomacy.

**Eligibility**

To be eligible for the scholarship, the applicant should meet the following requirements:

- The applicant should have excellent academic achievements that are relevant to the kind of course they are interested in. The applicant should rank amongst the top 10% for the relevant course.
- The applicant should not be a holder of EU/EEA Passport and should not also be eligible for support through loans and grants issued by the Dutch system.
- Students who have already obtained a Master's degree from Leiden University will not be eligible for the award apart from those who meet the requirement of two-year work experience.
- Before being awarded the scholarship, applicants will be required to submit in writing an agreement to the rules and regulations which is attached to the application form.
- Applicants who already have a bachelor's degree from Leiden University and intend to apply for Master's degree needs not to apply but can register directly.

- Applicants should also write a motivation letter with a maximum of 500 words where they state why they should be considered for the scholarship. The letter should be attached to the online application form.

**Scholarship's Value**

Leiden University Excellence Scholarship Program does not provide for full scholarship therefore arrangements should be made for additional funding that can take care of tuition and living expenses. The scholarship is only valid for the period the applicant is registered as a full time student with Leiden University.

The scholarship amount can either be €10,000 or 15,000 depending on the kind of award that one qualifies for.

The deadline for application for the scholarship is September.

- Application for Leiden University is done online where the online application form is filled.

- Once the form is filled you are required to upload all the required documents.
- When submitting your application, you should clearly indicate the kind of Master's program you are applying for and if you are applying for one or two.
- On the scholarship page you should also upload the scholarship motivation letter and then submit the form with all the necessary documents attached.
- You should then pay the €100 application fee.
- The applications will then be reviewed by the selected committee of the relevant faculty and applicants are selected based on academic merit.
- All the applicants will then be notified of the outcome by the scholarship department.

More information can be accessed at:

http://prospectivestudents.leiden.edu/scholarships/scholarship

# List of Scholarships for Studying in Australia

The Australian Government, organizations and Universities are known to provide International scholarship opportunities to scholars interested in pursuing higher education in Australia. The information shared here will give some insight on organizations and institutions in Australia that are offering either partial or full scholarship opportunities for Indian Nationalities.

## 1. Australian Awards Scholarships

Australian Awards Scholarships are long term development scholarships provided by the Australian Government under the Department of Foreign Affairs and Trade. The award is focused towards providing long term development needs of partner countries in accordance to the bilateral and regional agreements. People from developing countries like Asia, Africa, Pacific and Middle East are some of the beneficiaries of the award as they get the opportunity to undertake full time undergraduate or postgraduate study in some of the participating Australian Universities and colleges.

The selected applicants are expected to engage in research and study provided by the Australian Universities and is able to acquire knowledge and develop skills that help in driving change and contributing to the development outcomes of their specific countries.

## Scholarship Value and Details

The Australian Awards and Scholarships cover the following area:

- Full tuition fees
- Return Air Travel covering payment of economy class to and from Australia through the most direct route.
- A onetime payment of $5,000 as an establishment allowances that takes care of accommodation expenses, study materials and textbooks.

- A payment of $30,000 is made per year towards living expenses
- It also covers an introductory academic program which is a compulsory program that runs for 4-6 weeks before the commencement of the formal academic program. The introductory program is aimed towards covering information regarding living and studying in Australia.
- The award also takes care of the overseas student's health cover which covers basic medical costs for the period of the award.
- Supplementary academic support may also be provided to students that need to enhance their academic experience.
- Field work is compulsory and support may be given to research students.
- The study award amount may be up to $ 25,0000

**Eligibility**

- The award is open to citizens of countries in Asia, Middle East, Pacific and Africa with the list of countries being

India, Bangladesh, Pakistan, Papua New Guinea amongst others.

- The applicants are required to sign a contract with the commonwealth of Australia with a declaration that they will comply with all the requirements of the scholarship.
- After completion of the study period, the students are required to leave Australia for a period of two years and failure to comply may result into the student incurring a debt that is equivalent to the scholarship amount.
- The applicant should be of a minimum age of 18 years by the time of applying for the scholarship.
- The applicant should be a citizen of one of the listed countries and should be in their country at the time of submitting the application form.
- The applicant should not be married or be in a relationship with any person who might have Australian or New Zealand citizenship at the time of application.

- The applicant should not be in any way applying for another long-term Australian award.
- The applicant should be able to satisfy the necessary administration requirements of the University or institution that the study is to be undertaken.
- The applicant should be able to meet all the Department of Immigration requirements and Border Protection and be able to hold a Foreign Affairs (subclass 576) visa.
- The applicants should notify the Program Area of any relationship or connection to a staff or employee at Program Areas or with any managing contractors for a more transparent management of the application process.
- The deadline for the application form is 30th of April (for year 2017, though it varies from year to year)

To begin the application process goes to the Online Australia Scholarships Information Systems where you will register and get to respond to some questions. You will then be provided with a unique username, password and registration number. The information can be accessed through this link:

http://oasis.dfat.gov.au/

Once you begin the application process, you don't have to complete and send all the information at once, you can take time to update the information and ensure that all the necessary information is entered. Ensure that you submit all the information before the given deadline which is 30 of April. Once you have submitted the application, you will not be able to make any changes.

In case you find difficulty in applying online, you can as well make the applications through mail and contacts can be accessed through the Institution's website. The application form can be downloaded and filled and the necessary documents attached then sent to the provided contacts

For online application or downloading of the form, the information can be accessed at the website:

http://www.dfat.gov.au/people-to-people/australia-awards/Pages/australia-awards-scholarships.aspx

## 2. Endeavour Post Graduate Scholarships in Australia for International Students

The Endeavour Postgraduate Scholarships program provides awards to international students that are interested in pursuing postgraduate studies at a Masters' or PHD level either in research or coursework level in Australia for a period of four years. The studies can be undertaken in the higher education institutions or universities within Australia. The award is open to students from various developing countries including India.

**Scholarship Details and Value**

The scholarship includes various provisions like:

- Payment of tuition fees on a pro-rata basis for the entire period of research or study. The tuition fees also include the student's amenities and service fees.

- The duration of the scholarship is 2 years for Masters" Program and 4 years for PhD.
- The value of the award is $140, 500 for Master's program and $272, 500 for PhD program. The award also includes $AUD 3000 for travel expenses, $AUD 4,000 for establishment allowance and $AUD 3,000 monthly stipend. Travel and health insurance is also provided.

**Eligibility**

To be considered eligible for Endeavour Postgraduate Scholarship, the applicant should be able to meet the following requirements:

- The applicant should be of a minimum age of 18 years before the commencement of the program.
- The applicant should be a citizen of the participating nations and should be residing in the country at the time of sending the application.

- Should be able to provide all the required supporting documents
- The applicant should not submit application for a category that they have already completed the award with Endeavour Postgraduate Scholarship for.
- The list of countries that can participate include countries in Asia, The Caribbean, Pacific, Middle East amongst others.
- The applicants are required to attach a formal admission letter from the Australian college or university they intend to undertake their studies from.
- The deadline for submitting the application forms is 30th April
- All the applications are submitted electronically through Endeavour Online System and the required documents and other relevant information can be accessed from the website:

https://internationaleducation.gov.au/Endeavour%20program/Scholarships-and-Fellowships/Pages/default.aspx

### 3. Adelaide Scholarships International

The University of Adelaide awards international postgraduate students that have demonstrated high level of academic excellence in their academics. The award is for students undertaking Masters" Degree in Research or Doctoral Research Degree that is offered at the University. All the International students apart from citizens of New Zealand can submit applications.

### Scholarship Details and Value

The Adelaide Scholarships International provides course tuition fees to Masters" Degree students for a period of two years and Doctoral Research degree for three years. Apart from the tuition fee, the selected students are also provided with living allowance for the period of the program, visa fees, and overseas student health cover, world care policy that covers the students, their spouses and dependents.

The award does not cover the extended student visa period which is 6 months for post thesis submission. The award holder is expected to have subclass 500 visa and failure to hold that may result into them taking responsibility of health care costs.

The scholarship amount is $26,288

**Eligibility**

To be eligible for the scholarship, the applicants are expected to meet the following requirements:

- The applicant must have completed an academic qualification that is equivalent to Australian First Honors degree which mainly involves a four year degree program with a major research project undertaken in the final year. The applicant should be able to demonstrate successful completion of all the qualifying programs as scholarship is to be awarded in accordance to academic merit and the potential demonstrated in research.

- The international applicants should not by the time of application be holding research qualifications that are equivalent to the Australian Research Doctorate degree or if the applicant is undertaking A Masters' degree in Research, they should not hold a research qualification that is considered to be equivalent or higher than the Australian Research Master's degree.
- The applicants should be able to meet the required minimum proficiency in English language. Those applicants who will fail to provide proof of English proficiency will not be considered eligible for the scholarship.
- The applicants are required to enroll in the University as International students and should maintain the International student's status for the entire duration of their studies at the University.

- Applicants who are permanent citizens of Australia and New Zealand are not eligible for the scholarship. Applicants who have applied for Australian permanent residency can also apply.
- The applicant should not have any other award during the time of the scholarship or any knowledge of a student having another award or support will lead to cancellation of the scholarship.
- The deadline of the application for the scholarship is 30$^{th}$ April (of year 2017, though it varies from year to year)
- Applicants should submit a formal admission letter alongside scholarship application form through the online application system. The application forms and the required documents can be accessed from the institutions website where the applicant can begin by choosing the institution and the program to study. A research student handbook can then be downloaded and it is where all the requirements are stated. Once the applicant has read the

research student handbook, the necessary requirements can be put in place before continuing with the application process.

It is advisable that the applicant takes time to verify all the information filled for accuracy and consistency so that mistakes are avoided once the application is submitted.

## 4. La Trobe Academic Excellence Scholarships for International Students

La Trobe Academic Excellence Scholarships are for International students that have demonstrated high academic achievement and are interested in pursuing undergraduate and postgraduate programs in Australia. The scholarship is open to all International students from all countries apart from New Zealand. The scholarship only takes care of tuition fees and the applicant will be expected to cater for other expenses related to their study.

## Scholarship Details and Value

The value of the scholarship is between $10,000 and $20,000 and all is given towards tuition fees. The applicant is expected to make arrangements for any differences in fees, overseas student health cover, living expenses amongst others.

The award is submitted across a period of two semesters or 12 months and the student should attain an average of C grade if the scholarship is to be continued to the next year.

**Eligibility**

To be eligible for the award, the applicant should be able to meet the following requirements:

- The applicant should be a citizen of any other country apart from New Zealand or Australia and should be submitting application towards starting out as an undergraduate or postgraduate student.
- The applicant should demonstrate proof of having scored at least 85% in their previous tests or in their previous degree awards.

- The applicant should demonstrate proficiency in English language and can meet the entry requirements for the English language.
- An applicant is also considered not eligible if they are starting out for a higher degree by research, Diploma course, Foundation studies program, Study Abroad program and ELICOS.
- An applicant can apply if they already have an offer to study for an undergraduate or postgraduate program at the La Trobe University.
- The deadline for the scholarship is 9th of September
- Once the applicant has received an offer to join La Trobe University, they can go ahead and begin the process of application for scholarship. The application form can be downloaded from the University's website then filled and submitted through email to: intapplication@latrobe.edu.au

- The applicant should carefully read the downloaded application form and be able to fill in the correct information. It is advisable that all the details be verified before sending the forms through email.

More information can be accessed at:

http://www.latrobe.edu.au/scholarships

## 5. Monish International Merit Scholarships

Monash International Merit Scholarships is a program aimed at providing international students pursuing undergraduate and postgraduate degree at Monash University with an award that enables them to undertake outstanding coursework studies. International students from all the countries are encouraged to apply, however, preference is given to countries that have strategic priorities for Monash.

**Scholarship Details and Value**

The total average value of the scholarship for a five-year degree is up to about $50,000. An amount of $10,000 is awarded towards full time study per year for a study load of 48 credit points. Recipients of the scholarships may also be asked to take part in the Monash marketing and promotional events or recruitment.

**Eligibility**

- Selection to the university is based on academic achievement and applicants are required to have achieved 85% of the weighted average mark.
- Applicants should be international students and preference is given to those commencing their studies.
- To retain the scholarship the selected students should be able to score an average of 70% or above per semester.
- Applicants will be assessed on their application motivation statement which should be at least 500 words and their potential to be ambassadors for Monash University will be evaluated.

- Before submitting application for the scholarship, the applicant is expected to have received an offer letter from Monash University without any condition.
- The application process is different and mostly depends on the kind of coursework one is applying for. Ensure that you meet all the requirements before submitting your application. There are courses that have higher requirements for entry and for the undergraduate courses, the applicant should be below 17 years and should meet English proficiency requirements with one of the Australian or overseas qualification. The information for overseas or Australian qualifications can be accessed at the Institutions website.
- Other requirements may include admission tests, personal statements, curriculum vitae or resume, interviews amongst others. The information required for the application process can be accessed from the website and

the deadline for submitting application form is the 15th of October.

More information can be accessed at:

https://www.monash.edu/study/fees-scholarships/scholarships/find-a-scholarship?f.Citizenship|eligibilityCitizenship=International+student

## 6. IWC Masters' Scholarships for International Students

These are prestigious scholarships that are offered to high caliber applicants that have shown the potential of becoming future water leaders. The award is given to applicants who desire to pursue IWC Master of Integrated Water Management (MIWM) at the University of Queensland in Brisbane, Australia. The countries that are given priority for the scholarship are Asia-Pacific, Africa, Latin America and Middle East.

**Scholarship Value and Details**

- The scholarship is valued at an approximate amount of AU$92,645 and takes care of tuition fees
- They will be provided with a living expenses stipend that is valued at AU$36,000 for a period of 16 months and it is payable in equal monthly installments
- Provision of return air travel with an approved economy class air fare through the most direct route. The maximum amount payable for airfare is AU$2,500
- Provision of amenities fees and student services that is valued at AU$145
- Award towards cost of student visa that is valued at AU$550
- Award towards cost of Overseas Student Health Cover that is valued at AU$950 for a period of 18 months.

There is also a B type of scholarship that is offered to students from North America, Europe and Asia. The value for the type B scholarship is AU$52,500 and is to take care of full tuition fees.

Priority for the award is given to women who meet the requirements.

**Eligibility**

To be eligible for the scholarship, the applicant should be able to meet the following requirements:

- The applicant should have completed an undergraduate study from a recognized International University in a field of study that is related with the program being pursued.
- The applicant should have work experience of about two years either as a volunteer or paid work in a field that is relevant to the program.
- The applicant should also demonstrate proficiency in English language and should show proof of having attained the minimum score in TOEFL, IELTS or PTE tests.
- The applicant should be able to demonstrate leadership qualities, professional and volunteering record, excellent

academic record, commitments and potential of positive outcomes.

- The deadline for submitting application forms is 23$^{rd}$ of August and selected students will be notified through email by the 1$^{st}$ of November

- Application is done online and it is advisable that the applicant takes time to read the terms and conditions of the scholarship before submitting an application form. Once the applicants have submitted their application forms and are considered, they will be required to apply for admission at the MIWM program at the University of Queensland and those who have received an unconditional offer to join the University will be informed accordingly.

More information on how to go through the application process can be accessed at:

http://watercentre.org/master-of-integrated-water-management/tab/pillar4/

7. **UQ Bel India Scholarship**

This scholarship is awarded to students from India who are pursuing a Masters' degree coursework or an undergraduate degree in Economics and Law or Faculty of Business at the University of Queensland in Australia. The award of the scholarship is based on academic excellence and normally attracts students from the best learning institutions in India.

**Scholarship Value**

The scholarship award is offered in the form of tuition fee waiver where an amount equivalent to AUD 10,000 is waived. The final amount awarded to the winner is up to the discretion of the selection committee.

**Eligibility**

To be eligible for the award, the applicants should meet the following requirements:

- Applicants should be citizens of India who are residing in India.

- The applicant should have applied for admission to University of Queensland and should be having a letter of unconditional offer for a relevant course.
- The award is not available to students who are already studying in Australia.
- Applicants should be able to access application forms for the International students online.
- The applicants will then get a student ID issued by the University or Queensland and an unconditional offer.
- The applicant is also required to complete application forms for faculty of business economics and law.
- The deadline for the application is 30th October

More information can be accessed at:
https://scholarships.uq.edu.au/search/scholarships?f[0]=type%3Ascholarship&f[1]=field_nationality%3A2498&f[2]=field_enrolment_status%3A2362

## 8. Australia International Postgraduate Research Scholarships

This program provides International students with the opportunity to pursue postgraduate research studies in Australia as they get the experience of Australia's leading researchers. The studies can be undertaken in any of the participating universities in Australia. The areas of studies that the students are to engage in are Masters' degree research programs and Doctorate degree. The award is open to International students from all over the world apart from New Zealand.

The objective of IPRS program is to attract International postgraduates who are top quality students in the area of research and be able to support Australia's research efforts.

**Scholarship Value**

The full scholarship takes care of tuition fees, health insurance expenses and health insurance costs for dependents of the scholar. The scholarship is provided for a period of two years for those pursuing a Master's degree and three years for those pursuing doctorate degrees.

## Eligibility

To be eligible for the award, the applicant should be able to meet the following requirements:

- The applicant must be an international student except those from New Zealand who is starting a full-time higher degree research program at a university in Australia.
- The applicant should have proof of having completed a Bachelor's degree with first class honors or an equivalent level of attainment.
- The applicant should not be having another commonwealth funded scholarship award during the period of study.
- The application process and selection is carried differently by each University and the applicant should contact their chosen Universities scholarship office to find out on how they can apply for the scholarship.

- The deadline for submitting application forms vary depending on the University, however it is normally between April and October.

More information can be accessed at:

http://www.anu.edu.au/students/scholarships/australian-government-research-training-program-agrtp-international-fee-offsetresearch-training-program-agrtp-international-fee-offset

## 9. Flinders International Postgraduate Research Scholarships

This award is specifically provided towards support of international students that are undertaking a higher degree in research. The award is available to International countries apart from New Zealand. Consideration for the award is given to students who have demonstrated outstanding results in independent research and are willing to pursue their research doctorate degree at the Flinders University. The award is given in reference to the applicant's academic merit, research training and research indicators and performance.

## Scholarship Value

The scholarship takes care of full tuition fees, a generous living allowance of $26,288 an establishment allowance valued at $1,485 that takes care of relocation costs and airfare expenses. The award is available for three years for those undertaking Research Doctorate degree and two years for those undertaking Research Master's degree.

## Eligibility

To be eligible for the award, the applicant should be able to meet the following requirements:

- Applicants should be able to meet the University's academic entry requirements for the desired course whether it is a Master's degree or Doctorate Degree.

- Applicants are expected to have completed a course that is equivalent to an Australian First Class Honors degree. A four year degree program with a major research project in the final year.
- The applicant is expected to demonstrate proficiency in English language and be able to meet the levels of English proficiency standards set by the University for International students.
- Applicants should not be holders of a research degree qualification or an equivalent as the award is only available to those commencing their research degree programs.
- Applicants should not be holders of Australian citizenship, New Zealand citizenship or permanent residence status.
- The deadline for submitting the applications is 12th August.

More information can be accessed at:

http://www.flinders.edu.au/scholarships-system/index.cfm/scholarships/display/a731e2

# List of Scholarships for Studying in Canada

The number of scholarships that are available for international students in Canada is quite limited in comparison to those in the UK, Australia and the United States of America. However, there are a variety of organizations and institutions that offer partial and full time scholarship in Canada and you can get access to some of them here.

1. **York University International Student Scholarships**

The York University offers scholarships to international students that have shown exemplary academic excellence and are looking forward to pursuing full time undergraduate degree at the University of York. There are different types of scholarship offered by York University like the Global Leader of Tomorrow, United World College and International Entrance Scholarships. The field of study may include an undergraduate program that covers faculties like arts and media, environmental studies, Education, Health, Science and more.

**Scholarship Value and Details**

- The scholarship value for Global Leader of Tomorrow award is $68,000 for four years. ($17,000 x 4years)
- The award for United World College Scholarship is $112,000 for a period of four years. ($28,000 x 4 years)
- The International Entrance scholarship is $112,000 for four years. ($28,000 x 4 years)
- All the stated scholarships are renewable for a period of three years towards full time undergraduate study. The selected applicants are expected to demonstrate high levels of academic standing all through the academic years.

**Eligibility**

The following requirements should be met by the applicants if they are to be considered for the offer.

- The applicant should be an International student and is expected to be having a study permit to be able to study in Canada.
- The applicant should be directly from high school with no prior college or university study and should not have taken two years after graduating from high school.
- The applicant should have applied for an undergraduate program in any of the previously stated faculties or as shown in the institutions website.
- The applicant should be in possession of an excellent academic record which is an average of an 'A' or equivalent. The applicant should also show proof of demonstration of leadership qualities either through community service or in sports, arts, and other areas that express individual achievement.
- The applicant is expected to submit all the necessary documents including copies of academic transcripts,

language proficiency results, and GAP letters alongside the application forms.

- The deadline for the application is 15th of February
- Application is done online with the relevant documents submitted electronically. The application forms and required details can be accessed at the Universities official website: http://futurestudents.yorku.ca/funding#intl

## 2. University of Manitoba Graduate Fellowships

These are merit based awards offered to students of any nationality who are pursuing studies as full time Masters' students at the University of Manitoba. The students can apply for any graduate degree program that is offered in the University apart from Medicine and the faculty of Business Administration.

**Scholarship Value**

The value of the scholarship is $18,000 for PhD students and $12,000 for a Master's program and it covers a period of one year. The students are also eligible for the University of Manitoba

Graduate Fellowships award for a period of 24 months for those pursuing Masters' Courses and 48 months for those pursuing PhD courses.

**Eligibility**

- To be eligible for the award, students should have a minimum GPA score of 3.75 or B+ and above at a recognized University. The admissions criteria should be used in calculating GPA for example the last 60 credit hours or something equivalent to that.
- All students regardless of their citizenship are encouraged to apply for the scholarship provided they meet the requirements.
- Applicants should be able to contact the specific units for relevant information in regard to the requirements that is necessary when filling application forms, the documents required, availability of space within the unit and more.

Submitting an application without getting all the required unit guidelines may lead to failure.

- Application for scholarship is done electronically and the required information can be obtained from the specific units. Applying for the scholarship may take about 30 minutes however it is advisable that you have all the required documents ready and in soft copy at the time of application. The documents can then be directly uploaded or you can decide to submit your application through the post, in such a case, you will have to enclose the documents in a sealed casing.
- It is advisable that you don't submit the application form immediately as you may still need to make the necessary editing or add any information that may come up. All you have to do once you update your is to save the changes then log in later when using your unique username and password. Check your application thoroughly before

submission given you will not be able to make any changes once it is submitted.

- The online application fee is $100 and if you are sending the application forms and documents through post then you will be required to pay $120.

Just to ensure that the whole application process goes on well, ensure that you have the following in place before beginning the application process:

i. Get information on department's application requirements and familiarize yourself with them.

ii. Secure the necessary arrangements with your advisor if need be.

iii. Put together all your transcripts and get them scanned and available in soft copy.

iv. Put together all the necessary test scores that are relevant for your application.

v. Verify all the requirements and just ascertain if you have all that is required.

vi. Contact potential referees and get their recommendations.

vii. Click the apply now button and fill your application form

The deadline for submitting application formal varies annually and you can keep on checking to ensure you don't miss out.

For more information regarding the scholarship check out the Institutions website:

http://umanitoba.ca/faculties/graduate_studies/funding/585.html

## 3. University of Alberta Centenary Scholarship

This scholarship is awarded to international students who have demonstrated superior academic achievement and are pursuing undergraduate degree program at the University of Alberta. Selection criteria are mainly based on the applicant's academic standing, leadership qualities that include involvement in extracurricular activities and community services.

## Scholarship Value

The scholarships offered by the University of Alberta are several and the value of the scholarship ranges from $3,000 to $40,000 and is payable over a period of four years.

## Eligibility

International students from all countries are eligible for the scholarship.

The receipt of funding for the subsequent years is dependent on the achievement of a minimum GPA of 3.5 for a full term normal course load for each year.

- Before submitting application for the scholarship, the applicant should first attain an admission for a degree program at the University of Alberta. Once the admission letter is received, the applicant will be given a CCID and password that can be used to log in online and get to access the application form for the scholarship.

- There are documents that should also be submitted together with the application form like the academic transcripts that shows the completed courses and the grades achieved, documents showing proof of English proficiency, recommendation letters and contacts of the references as they will be contacted.
- The training is to be carried out in Canada and the deadline for the scholarship is 15th of December.

More information can be accessed at:
https://www.ualberta.ca/admissions/international/tuition-and-scholarships/scholarships-and-awards/country-specific-scholarships

## Vanier Canada Graduate Scholarships

The Vanier Canada graduate scholarship is organized by the Canadian government with the aim of attracting and retaining doctoral students that are outstanding and be able to project Canada as the global centre of excellence in regard to higher learning and research programs. The applicants are selected in reference to demonstration of high standards of academic achievements, leadership skills and achievement in extracurricular activities and other areas.

There are three types of scholarships offered by Vanier Canada Graduate and the scholarships are evenly distributed amongst the three federal granting agencies.

The agencies include:

i. Canadian Institute of health research (CIHR)
ii. Natural Sciences and Engineering Research Council (NSERC)
iii. Social Sciences and Humanities Research Council (SSHRC)

**Eligibility**

To be eligible for the award, applicants should be able to meet the following requirements:

- Vanier Canada scholarship is available to Canadian students and foreign students from other countries.

- The applicant should be pursuing their first doctoral degree which may also include a joint undergraduate and graduate research program.
- The applicant should have the intention of pursuing full time doctoral studies and research at the chosen institution.
- The applicant must not be holding a doctoral level scholarship from any of the three granting agencies at the time of submitting application.
- The applicant should be having an admission from one Canadian Institution that must have already received a Vanier CGS quota.
- For the students that are registered for joint undergraduate and graduate degree programs, the undergraduate portion of the program will not be factored towards the number of months to be completed for doctoral levels.

- Applicants can make direct applications to Vanier Canada Graduate Scholarship and the agency specific scholarships.

**Scholarship Value**

The value of the scholarship is $50,000 per year and covers a period of three years which is nonrenewable.

- Before starting off the application process the applicant should take time and verify the institution they intend to submit their application for doctoral studies to and if they have a Vanier CGS quota.
- Submission of the application form is done electronically through ResearchNet and the applicant should start by first completing the Vanier CGS electronic form which is then submitted the respective Canadian Institution that is to nominate the student for scholarship.
- Application for the scholarship is done in two ways, the applicant can either inform the faculty of graduate studies

of the desired institution through which they intend to apply for the Vanier CGS program or the institution can decide to directly nominate the applicant directly.

- Application forms are then filled using the ResearchNet application system and then submitted by the applicant to the nominating institution.
- The applicants can then follow up with the respective institutions for more information regarding selection of the right federal granting agency and any other inquires related to the application process.
- The deadline for submitting the applications is 2nd of November.

More information regarding the scholarship can be obtained from the website:

http://www.vanier.gc.ca/en/nomination_process-processus_de_mise_en_candidature.html

5. **Banting Postdoctoral Fellowships**

Banting Postdoctoral fellowships provides awards to some of the best postdoctoral applicants with the focus of contributing to the country's social, economic and research based growth. The objective of the fellowship is to attract and retain top postdoctoral talent at both national and international level. The focus is also towards enabling the

applicants to develop leadership potential as they position themselves as research leaders of tomorrow.

**Scholarship Value**

The value of the scholarship is $70,000 per year for a period of two years.

**Eligibility**

- The applicant is expected to complete the application forms alongside that of the host institution.

- The applicant is expected to show commitment to the research program and should be in alignment with the institution's strategic priorities.
- The merit of the applicant will be a determinant towards eligibility including their ability to launch a successful career that is research intensive.
- The deadline for submitting application forms is 21$^{st}$ of September.
- Before you start off the application process ensure that you read the application guide before applying. The applicants are required attain an average score of 5.1 in all the three areas. The application should be written with a non-specialist research approach in mind as the selection committee is a multidisciplinary one.
- The applicant should ensure that the application is fully complete including admission letter from the university the applicant intends to undertake to carry out the

research from. The applicant should also include all the necessary academic documents.

Information regarding the scholarship can be accessed from: [http://banting.fellowships-bourses.gc.ca/en/home-accueil.html](http://banting.fellowships-bourses.gc.ca/en/home-accueil.html)

6. **University of Calgary Graduate Awards**

The University of Calgary offers awards to International students that have demonstrated scholastic achievement in their field of study. The award can either be partial or full scholarship and they are quite competitive. The applicants are encouraged to explore all the award options and settle for that which they feel best addresses their academic and financial needs. Some of the awards offered under the University of Calgary include: Alberta Innovates that addresses health solutions, Alberta Innovates for Technology features, Graduate Award Competition. Doctoral Recruitment scholarships and Vanier Canada Graduate Scholarships.

## Scholarship Value

The value of the scholarship may range from $1,000 to $40,000.

## Eligibility

- Application must be made for the graduate awards as no one will be automatically considered. Application for the award can be made after submission of application to the University for admission and student number is obtained.
- You don't have to wait until you are accepted for the program in order to apply for the award.
- Students with other sources of funding are not eligible for the award.
- You are considered an International student if you are in Canada to pursue studies for a limited period of time then get to return back to your country. You are also an International student if you are not a citizen of Canada or have permanent residency.

- The deadline for submitting application forms is 1st of May

More information can be accessed at:

http://grad.ucalgary.ca/awards/award-opportunities/university-awards

### 7. Fincad Women in Finance Scholarship

Fincad scholarship is focused towards supporting and encouraging women who have shown exemplary achievements in the field of finance and leadership. The award is for graduate level programs in finance specifically and related to areas like financial risk management, derivatives in capital markets and more. Fincad is aware of the fact that majority of the players in the financial industry are men and that's the reason the scholarship is open to women of any age as long as they meet the requirements.

**Scholarship Value**

The value of Fincad scholarship is US$ 10,000 which is given towards support of graduate level studies.

**Eligibility**

- The application is open to women who have demonstrated high levels of achievement and meets all the requirements for the award.
- The application is also open to women of any age and citizenship
- Access to application forms and relevant documents can be done online through the institutions website and it is advisable that the applicant get to read and understand all the requirements and necessary details before starting off the application process. Ensure that you have all the necessary documents in place before submitting the application form.

The deadline for the application process is 26th of February and extra information can be accessed from the Institutions website:

http://www.fincad.com/about-fincad/corporate-information/scholarship

## 8. PEO International Peace Scholarships for Women.

This is a program that is focused towards providing selected women with awards to enable them undertake graduate study in Canada. The studies can be carried out at the accredited Universities and colleges within Canada. The levels of study include a Masters' or a PhD program in any field of study. The scholarships are given as grants in aid and do not take care of all the personal and academic expenses.

**Scholarship Value**

The value of the scholarship is a maximum amount of $12,500 per year and lower amounts may be awarded depending on the applicants need.

**Eligibility**

To be eligible for the scholarship, one should be able to meet the following requirements:

- The applicant should be qualified for a full time graduate study and should also be working towards attaining a graduate degree in any of the accredited colleges or universities in Canada.
- An applicant who is a citizen of the United States or Canada is not eligible for the scholarship.
- To be able to qualify for the first scholarship, the applicant should at least be remaining with a full year worth of coursework and should be enrolled and be in the institution full time for the rest of the study period.
- Doctoral students who have already completed their coursework and are only remaining with dissertations are not eligible to apply for the scholarship.
- Eligibility by the applicant to apply for the offer should be first established before the actual application form is submitted.

- The deadline for submitting application forms alongside other documents is the 15$^{th}$ of September.

Before submitting the application forms, applicants are first vetted to ensure they select programs that they are qualified to apply for. The form to be field before the vetting process begins can be accessed online from the website.

Once the courses you intend to register for are approved then you will be granted access to the online application form where you can then submit your application form and relevant documents.

More information can be accessed at:

http://www.peointernational.org/about-peo-international-peace-scholarship-ip

# World Bank / International Loans (Other Global organizations) that give Education Loans to Developing Economies

Even though this is a book of scholarships, we do have additional information on student loans. The reason for this is that there are too many students who have succumbed to scams in the market regarding scams / pay-day-loans etc. While we definitely recommend trying to get a full scholarship, the below options are a lot better than predatory pay day loan companies in the United States.

- **Credila Financial Services**

This loan is currently backed by one of the largest mortgage holders inside of India and is specifically meant for India citizens to study abroad. This loan comes with a 10-year plan for paying it back and only applies to Indian citizens. All loans provided by Credila on educational purposes must have collateral signed over to the company and extensive documentation proving that you will be attending a college that is outside of India and that you will be attending a college is required by Credila.

- **Global Student Loan Corporation**

This loan is applicable to those who do not have a United States citizen to co-sign for the student and, therefore, is applicable to anyone in the world. You do have to locate one of the approved schools that will accept this alone and while there are over 30 different schools that accept the loan, there are schools that do not and that maybe one of your schools.

- **Citizens Bank Student Loan**

This loan is based in the United States and does require a United States cosigner in order to be seen for approval. Once approved, the loan can be used in whichever school you may be attending in the United States. The amount of money that is approved for you will depend upon the credit of the individual who is co-signing for you. This means that you can get enough to pay for your entire education or enough to pay for a single year of your education or even less depending on whoever is co-signing for you.

- **Prodigy Finance**

This business provides loans to MBA students seeking to further their education within the United States. While they do loan out to individuals who do not have American co-signers, the number of universities that accept this loan is very small so unless you are an MBA student that will go to one of these colleges, their loan will likely be of no use to you.

- **Mpower Finance**

You do not have to have a cosigner with this company in order to obtain a loan as they are not only based in the United States but also inside of India. They are a relatively new company in the student loans market and so their approval for universities is still rather low. This is one of the rare companies that will only let you know where you can apply the loan after you have applied for the loan.

- **Stilt Inc.**

Stilt is one of the biggest student loan lenders that will lend to those that do not have an American cosigner. They are not selective in what degrees that they will loan for and their loan can be used for non-tuition purposes also. This means that their loan can be utilized for living expenses, eating out at a restaurant, or whatever you want that you can apply the money towards. However, they will not loan you more than $25,000, which does not cover some of the more expensive college degrees.

- **Avanse**

This company does require an American cosigner in order to obtain the loan and you do have to have a school that approves of this loan before it can be utilized. Outside of school tuition, this loan is not applicable to any other thing that you might need. The loan is not degree specific and it does come with very low interest rates over the years.

- **ReliaMax**

This is another loan that you do not have to have an American cosigner for and it will depend on what you are applying for as to how much credit they will give you on your loan. This loan is only to be used for schools within the United States.

- **Sallie Mae**

Sallie Mae is one of the largest lenders when it comes to student loans and has several different programs depending on who you are, what you're studying and where you're studying it. This means that you could get a relatively small amount of money or you could get a massive pile of money in order to pay for your studies and where you're studying at. Sallie Mae is also one of the rare lenders that can be applied towards International universities outside the United States. There will be a minimum of a $1,000 loan and you will get an advisor that will help you go through which loans are best for you. Depending on what you are applying for, you may or may not need a co-signer in order to provide the credit level to get what you are applying for. This means that you may or may not get the loan that you need. Unlike many of the lenders that will try to get you to loan as much as you can, Sallie Mae will warn you several times on their main website that you should only borrow exactly what you need and no more than that.

- **New Hampshire Education Loan Corporation**

You will need a cosigner for this loan. You can defer this loan rather than begin paying it off straight away while you are in school but it will cost you more in the long run. You can also defer the payments if you can prove that you are suffering an economic hardship but this only lasts for up to a year.

- **Union Federal Private Student Loan funded by SunTrust Bank**

You will need a cosigner for this loan but one of the benefits to this specific loan is that you can get a reduction over the overall amount that you owe by graduating the college. Additionally, this is one of the rare loans that you can apply loan forgiveness to if you become applicable for it. Additional to that is the fact that you can defer this loan rather than begin paying it off straight away but it will cost you more in the long run.

# Reliable sources for loans in India

- **United Bank of India**

In order to obtain a loan from this lender, you have to be an Indian national. Additionally, you will need to pass the entrance exam before you can apply for this loan. The lender will give you a maximum of 10 lakhs for local study and a maximum of 20 lakhs for study abroad. You will have a 4-7 year repayment period depending on the size of your loan. While the company may have multiple loans to provide you with, there's usually a 12-13% interest.

- **SBI Education Loan**

This lender has a large and wide variety of varying loans that it can provide you for educational purposes. Not only can the loan be utilized for educational purposes, but this lender will allow you to utilize the loan for extraneous purposes such as travel costs and living expenses. The lender will give you a maximum of

10 lakhs for local study and a maximum of 30 lakhs for study abroad.

- **Punjab National Bank Saraswati**

This lender has a large and wide variety of varying loans that it can provide you for educational purposes. In order to obtain a loan from this lender, you have to be an Indian national. The lender will give you a maximum of 10 lakhs for local study and a maximum of 20 lakhs for study abroad. While the company may have multiple loans to provide you with, there's usually a 10-15% interest. This is one of the few companies that will require collateral whenever you are attempting to obtain a loan from them.

- **IDBI Bank**

The lender will give you a maximum of 10 lakhs for local study and a maximum of 20 lakhs for study abroad. While the company may have multiple loans to provide you with, there's usually a 10-14% interest.

- **Canara Bank's Education Loan**

This lender has a large and wide variety of varying loans that it can provide you for educational purposes. The lender will give you a maximum of 10 lakhs for local study and a maximum of 20 lakhs for study abroad. While the company may have multiple loans to provide you with, there's usually a 10-13% interest.

- **Mpower Finance**

They are a relatively new company in the student loans market and so their approval for universities is still rather low. This is one of the rare companies that will only let you know where you can apply the loan after you have applied for the loan.

- **Credila Financial Services**

This loan is currently backed by one of the largest mortgage holders inside of India and is specifically meant for India citizens to study abroad. All loans provided by Credila on educational purposes must have collateral signed over to the company and extensive documentation proving that you will be attending a college that is outside of India is required by Credila.

- **Bank of India's Student Education Loan**

This lender has a large and wide variety of varying loans that it can provide you for educational purposes. The lender will give you a maximum of 10 lakhs for local study and a maximum of 20 lakhs for study abroad. In order to obtain a loan from this lender, you have to be an Indian national. Additionally, you will need to pass the entrance exam before you can apply for this loan. While the company may have multiple loans to provide you with, there's usually a 12-13% interest.

- **Dena Vidyalaxmi Education Loan**

This lender has a large and wide variety of varying loans that it can provide you for educational purposes. The lender will give you a maximum of 10 lakhs for local study and a maximum of 20 lakhs for study abroad.

- **Vijaya Bank's Student Loan**

This lender has a large and wide variety of varying loans that it can provide you for educational purposes. The lender will give you a maximum of 10 lakhs for local study and a maximum of 20 lakhs for study abroad. While the company may have multiple loans to provide you with, there's usually a 11-13% interest.

- **Sallie Mae**

Depending on the type of student you are, where you are located, and what you are studying, you may or may not be able to get a loan from Sallie Mae. Sallie Mae covers a wide variety of different loans and is an international lender that generally is applicable to most undergraduates, graduates, and individuals seeking to be certified in specialty skills. While Sally may not be based in side of India, Sallie Mae does provide students in India with loans for educational purposes.

- **Allahabad Bank**

This lender has a large and wide variety of varying loans that it can provide you for educational purposes. Additionally, you will need to pass the entrance exam before you can apply for this loan. The lender will give you a maximum of 50 lakhs for study abroad. While the company may have multiple loans to provide you with, there's usually a 11-12% interest.

- **Axis Bank**

This lender has a large and wide variety of varying loans that it can provide you for educational purposes. The lender will give you a maximum of 10 lakhs for local study and a maximum of 20 lakhs for study abroad. While the company may have multiple loans to provide you with, there's usually a 11-13% interest.

- **HDFC Education Loan**

This lender has a large and wide variety of varying loans that it can provide you for educational purposes. The lender will give you a maximum of 10 lakhs for study abroad. While the company may have multiple loans to provide you with, there's usually a 9-16% interest.

- **Axis Bank Education Loan**

This lender has a large and wide variety of varying loans that it can provide you for educational purposes. The lender will give you a maximum of 20 lakhs or more depending on the necessity. While the company may have multiple loans to provide you with, there's usually a 16-17% interest.

- **Avanse Education Loan**

This lender has a large and wide variety of varying loans that it can provide you for educational purposes. Not only can the loan be utilized for educational purposes, but this lender will allow you to utilize the loan for extraneous purposes such as travel cost and living expenses. There is no actual limit to how much you can borrow from this lender, but they will give you a set amount when you apply. While the company may have multiple loans to provide you with, there's usually an interest rate that is not set in stone.

- **Syndicate Bank**

This lender has a large and wide variety of varying loans that it can provide you for educational purposes. Not only can the loan be utilized for educational purposes, but this lender will allow you to utilize the loan for extraneous purposes such as travel cost and living expenses. The lender will give you a maximum of 20 lakhs for study abroad. While the company may have multiple loans to provide you with, there's usually a 11-13% interest.

- **State Bank of Mysore**

This lender has a large and wide variety of varying loans that it can provide you for educational purposes. Not only can the loan be utilized for educational purposes, but this lender will allow you to utilize the loan for extraneous purposes such as travel cost and living expenses. The lender will give you a maximum of 20 lakhs for study abroad. While the company may have multiple loans to provide you with, there's usually an interest rate that is not set in stone.

- **Dena Bank Education Loan**

This lender has a large and wide variety of varying loans that it can provide you for educational purposes. Not only can the loan be utilized for educational purposes, but this lender will allow you to utilize the loan for extraneous purposes such as travel cost and living expenses. The lender will give you a maximum of 10 lakhs for local study and a maximum of 20 lakhs for study abroad. While the company may have multiple loans to provide you with, there's usually a 13% interest.

- **Dhanalakshmi Bank Education Loan**

This lender has a large and wide variety of varying loans that it can provide you for educational purposes. Not only can the loan be utilized for educational purposes, but this lender will allow you to utilize the loan for extraneous purposes such as travel cost and living expenses. The bank will set the limit of how much you can borrow but there is no preset limitation. While the company may have multiple loans to provide you with, there's usually a 13-16% interest. This is one of the few companies that will require collateral whenever you are attempting to obtain a loan from them.

- **Federal Bank Education Loan**

This lender has a large and wide variety of varying loans that it can provide you for educational purposes. Not only can the loan be utilized for educational purposes, but this lender will allow you to utilize the loan for extraneous purposes such as travel cost and living expenses. In order to obtain a loan from this lender, you have to be an Indian national. The lender will give you a maximum of 10 lakhs for local study and a maximum of 20 lakhs for study abroad. While the company may have multiple loans to provide you with, there's usually a 13-16% interest.

- **Indian Bank Education Loan**

This lender has a large and wide variety of varying loans that it can provide you for educational purposes. Not only can the loan be utilized for educational purposes, but this lender will allow you to utilize the loan for extraneous purposes such as travel cost and living expenses. The lender will give you a maximum of 15 lakhs for local study and a maximum of 25 lakhs for study abroad. While the company may have multiple loans to provide you with, there's usually a 13% interest. This is one of the few companies that will require collateral whenever you are attempting to obtain a loan from them.

- **Karur Vysya Bank Education Loan**

This lender has a large and wide variety of varying loans that it can provide you for educational purposes. Not only can the loan be utilized for educational purposes, but this lender will allow you to utilize the loan for extraneous purposes such as travel cost and living expenses. In order to obtain a loan from this lender, you have to be an Indian national. The lender will give you a maximum of 10 lakhs for local study and a maximum of 20 lakhs for study abroad. While the company may have multiple loans to provide you with, there's usually a 13-16% interest. This is one of the few companies that will require collateral whenever you are attempting to obtain a loan from them.

- **Lakshmi Vilas Bank Education Loan**

This lender has a large and wide variety of varying loans that it can provide you for educational purposes. Not only can the loan be utilized for educational purposes, but this lender will allow you to utilize the loan for extraneous purposes such as travel cost and living expenses. In order to obtain a loan from this lender, you have to be an Indian national. The lender will give you a maximum of 10 lakhs for local study and a maximum of 20 lakhs for study abroad. While the company may have multiple loans to provide you with, there's usually a 13-16% interest. This is one of the few companies that will require collateral whenever you are attempting to obtain a loan from them.

- **Oriental Bank of Commerce Education Loan**

This lender has a large and wide variety of varying loans that it can provide you for educational purposes. Not only can the loan be utilized for educational purposes, but this lender will allow you to utilize the loan for extraneous purposes such as travel cost and living expenses. In order to obtain a loan from this lender, you have to be an Indian national. The lender will give you a maximum of 10 lakhs for local study and a maximum of 20 lakhs for study abroad. While the company may have multiple loans to provide you with, there's usually a 13-16% interest. This is one of the few companies that will require collateral whenever you are attempting to obtain a loan from them.

# Developed countries (with GDP per capita > $25000) with lowest education cost

- **Norway: Free**

Norway has to go at the top of this list because it's free and there's nothing cheaper than free. The best part about being free in this situation is that you don't get the full downside of something that you usually get free, which is to say that products that are usually free come with a downside of quality; but since Norway Prides itself on quality education, the education is great.

- **France: $200-$500 per year**

France has to be second this list because it is almost free in comparison to a lot of the prices that are associated with college costs. France is not only a great center for education but it's also a great area for tourism, which means that there are a variety of individuals intermingling throughout the country and this boosts the value of the education from France. However, due to the fact that this is France and a lot of tourists stop inside of France, the living expenses for the areas near Paris, a common place where people seek education, is rather high compared to the surrounding European countries.

- **California: University of the People: $2,000 for Associates Degree**

University of the People is based in California but you don't have to be in California in order to be a student of University of the People. The expenses of normal California colleges are very high and the only reason why California is on this list is due to University of the People being based in side of California. University of the People has an Associates program and a Bachelor program with the Associate program costing $2,000 while the Bachelor program costs $4,000. University of the People is limited in what it can teach you and it only has three different degrees at the time of writing this book. University of the People provides a medical degree, a business degree, and a computer science degree.

- **Poland: $2,000-$3,000 per year**

Poland is a small nation and this is beneficial for two different reasons. First, Poland has one of the cheapest rates when it comes to colleges and second, Poland also has one of the cheapest living rates when it comes to living around the colleges that you plan to attend. You can stay inside of Poland for less than $10,000 a year around the colleges that you want to be at. This makes it extremely cheap in comparison to some of the other colleges on this list. Additionally, due to the size of the country, transportation costs are significantly lower in areas such as the United States of America and Argentina.

- **Taiwan: $3,000-$4,000 per year**

Taiwan not only has one of the cheapest educational rates but also serves as an important technology hub for the world. A good portion of integrated circuits and other printed circuit board components come from Taiwan, which is why the computer science educational system in this country is highly sought-after. Not only can you learn computer science at a very cheap rate but you can immediately find available work, which is rare in a lot of these countries. Additionally, Taiwan is a generally cheap area to live in.

- **Germany: $10,000-$11,000 per degree**

Germany has a strong educational system that brings in a lot of international students. The undergraduate and PhD students of universities often have no tuition fees attached to their education. Additionally, the living expenses for being inside of Germany is usually in between the range of $9,000 to $12,000 depending per year on how you live. Those who are studying for their Bachelor's or their Master's degree can expect to pay around $5,000 to $10,000 over the course of their education. This educational cost can usually be covered by a scholarship of some type and Germany reinforces education to be more English-centric than some of the other countries on this list by having a wide range of in-university or out-of-university courses on English. This makes Germany, even though it is the highest in cost on this list, very inviting to internationally bound students.

| \multicolumn{4}{c}{Scholarships} | | | |
|---|---|---|---|
| Name | Eligible For | Max Reward | University or Country Applicable |
| CT Minority Teacher Incentive Grant Program | Connecticut Undergraduates | $5000 | USA |
| APSA Minority Fellows Program | All Minorities | $2000 | U.S.A. |
| Indiana University-Bloomington National Hispanic Scholarship | US High School Students | $1000 | Indiana University |
| P.E.O. International Peace Scholarship Fund | U.S. or Canadian students and non-students | $10000 | U.S. and Canada |
| Florida Minority Teacher Education Scholarship Program | Florida Undergraduates | $4000 | U.S.A. |
| Adoph Van Pelt Scholarship | U.S. Undergraduates | $1500 | U.S.A. |
| Sequoyah Graduate Scholarship | Anyone Seeking A Master's Degree | $1500 | Federally Recognized Native American Schools |
| Florence Young Memorial Scholarship | Students seeking a degree in Art, Law, | $1500 | Federally Recognized Native American Schools |

| | | | |
|---|---|---|---|
| Minority Dental Student Scholarship Program | Students Entering Second Year of Dental School | $2500 | U.S.A. |
| Airbus Leadership Grant | Students who have a GPA above 3.0 in their sophomore year or while currently pursuing an aviation degree | $5000 | U.S.A. |
| Live Your Dream: Education and Training Awards for Women | Women Members of Soroptimist International | $10000 | International |
| Penobscot Nation Fellowship | Penobscot Nation graduates | $750 | Circumstantial |
| Penobscot Nation Higher Education Grant Program | Penobscot Nation undergraduates | $1200 | Circumstantial |
| United Parcel Service Scholarship for Minority Students | minority undergraduate students to graduate by May/June 2018 or later | $4000 | U.S. |

| William Randolph Hearst Endowed Fellowship for Minority Students | Minority students in the social sciences | $4000 | U.S. |
|---|---|---|---|
| Clemson University Diversity Scholarships | undergraduates | $6000 | Clemson University Diversity |
| UPS Diversity Scholarship | college juniors in occupational safety and health | $5250 | U.S. |
| Thompson Scholarship for Women in Safety | female graduate in safety engineering | $1000 | U.S. |
| James Joseph Davis Memorial Scholarship | undergraduate students in occupational safety and health | $10000 | U.S. |
| AAUW International Fellowship | full-time study women who are not U.S. citizen | $30000 | U.S. |
| CIRI General Semester Scholarship | U.S. undergraduate or graduate students | $2500 | U.S. |

| | | | |
|---|---|---|---|
| William Randolph Hearst Endowed Fellowship for Minority Students | Minority students in the social sciences | $4000 | U.S. |
| Clemson University Diversity Scholarships | undergraduates | $6000 | Clemson University Diversity |
| UPS Diversity Scholarship | college juniors in occupational safety and health | $5250 | U.S. |
| Thompson Scholarship for Women in Safety | female graduate in safety engineering | $1000 | U.S. |
| James Joseph Davis Memorial Scholarship | undergraduate students in occupational safety and health | $10000 | U.S. |
| AAUW International Fellowship | full-time study women who are not U.S. citizen | $30000 | U.S. |
| CIRI General Semester Scholarship | U.S. undergraduate or graduate students | $2500 | U.S. |

| | | | |
|---|---|---|---|
| Florida Library Association Minority Scholarship Fund | U.S. undergraduate or graduate students in the minority | $2000 | U.S. |
| AAUW Career Development Grant | full-time study women who are not U.S. citizen seeking Bachelor's | $12000 | U.S. |
| Kathy Johnson Outreach Scholarship | non-traditional undergraduate or post-baccalaureate | $600 | U.S. |
| Harriet Evelyn Wallace Scholarship | graduate women studying geological science | $5000 | U.S. |
| AAUW Selected Professions Fellowships | full-time study women who are not U.S. citizen seeking Masters' | $18000 | U.S. |
| Holly A. Cornell Scholarship | U.S. Female and/or minority working on Master's | $7500 | U.S. |

| | | | |
|---|---|---|---|
| Dave Caldwell Scholarship | female and minority undergraduate majoring in engineering | $10000 | U.S. |
| Pride Foundation Associates in Behavioral Health Scholarship | gay, lesbian, or transgendered undergraduates | $3300 | U.S. |
| Porter Physiology Development Fellowship | minority graduate students working on Ph. D. in physiology | $28300 | U.S. |
| Annual Diversity Scholarship | first-year law school students of an oppressed diverse population | $15000 | U.S. |
| New York Women in Communications Foundation College Scholarship | Female college seeking students | $10000 | U.S. (New York) |
| ASA Minority Fellowship Program | Applicants in a program that | $18000 | U.S. |

| | | | |
|---|---|---|---|
| | grants a PHD in sociology | | |
| Royce Osborn Minority Student Scholarship | U.S. minority undergraduate students in entry-level radiograph course career | $4000 | U.S. |
| Ka'iulani Home for Girls Trust Scholarship | 1. female college freshmen and sophomores 2. residents of Hawaii | $739 | Hawaii |
| Ambassador Minerva Jean Falcon Hawai'i Scholarship | undergraduate and graduate students | $750 | Hawaii |
| Blossom Kalama Evans Memorial Scholarship Fund | 1. female college freshmen and sophomores 2. residents of Hawaii | $1166 | Hawaii |
| Financial Women International Scholarship | female college freshmen and sophomores | $2000 | International |

| | | | | |
|---|---|---|---|---|
| | pursuing financial careers | | | |
| Thz Fo Farm Scholarship Fund | 1. female college freshmen and sophomores 2. residents of Hawaii 3. Gerontology studies | $1833 | | Hawaii |
| ASM Minority Undergraduate Research Fellowship | 1. ASM member U.S. Citizen or permanent resident full-time undergraduate in a research project have an ASM mentor 2. Not receive financial support for research during the fellowship. | $4000 | | Circumstantial |

| | | | |
|---|---|---|---|
| Rukmini and Joyce Vasudevan Scholarship | Wisconsin female medical students entering their third or fourth year | $5000 | Wisconsin |
| Kappa Epsilon-AFPE-Nellie Wakeman First Year Graduate School Scholarship | members of Kappa Epsilon in the final year of pharmacy college | $7500 | U.S. |
| Zeta Phi Beta General Graduate Scholarship | international women and U.S. women | $2500 | Circumstantial |
| Nancy B. Woolridge McGee Graduate Fellowship | members of Zeta Phi Beta enrolled full time | $1000 | Circumstantial |
| Mildred Cater Bradham Social Work Fellowship | members of Zeta Phi Beta enrolled full time | $1000 | Circumstantial |
| Calvin College A.M.D.G. Scholarship | International and U.S. college sophomores, juniors and/or seniors | $2300 | International |
| Jackie Robinson Scholarship | U.S. minority high school seniors with an SAT score of 1000 | $7000 | U.S. |

| | | | |
|---|---|---|---|
| Curry Award for Girls and Young Women | U.S. undergraduate and/or graduate young women who are 16 to 26 years | $1000 | U.S. |
| Kahdine Ann DaCosta Scholarship for Excellence in Leadership | minority high school seniors attending an inner-city school | $1000 | U.S. |
| National Press Club Scholarship for Journalism Diversity | international and U.S. minority high school seniors | $2500 | U.S. |
| ACS Scholars Program | senior and college undergraduate minority students with a grade point average of 3.0 | $5000 | U.S. |
| Ruth Peterson Fellowship for Racial and Ethnic Diversity | graduate students pursuing a PhD in criminology. | $6000 | U.S. |
| UNC-Greensboro Alice McArver Ratchford Scholarship | undergraduate female students at UNC-Greensboro | $1000 | U.S. |
| P. O. Pistilli Scholarship | high school seniors planning to major in electrical engineering | $4000 | U.S. |
| VSGC Undergraduate STEM Bridge Scholarship | his award is for U.S college sophomores who are enrolled full time in a | $1000 | |

|  |  | program of study in science |  |  |
|---|---|---|---|---|
| Enterprise Holdings Scholarship | | 16 years of age or older | $5000 | U.S. |
| PepsiCo Scholarship | | 16 years of age or older | $5000 | U.S. |
| UPS Scholarship | | 16 years of age or older | $5000 | U.S. |
| Bruce Lee Scholarship | | 16 years of age or older | $5000 | U.S. |
| Leonard M. Perryman Communications Scholarship | | United Methodist ethnic minority student | $2500 | U.S. |
| Gertrude B. Elion Mentored Medical Student Research Award | | U.S. female medical students | $10000 | U.S. |
| Helen M. Clymer Scholarship | | undergraduate students of Berks County, Pennsylvania | $2361 | U.S. |
| The Marie A. Calderilla Scholarship | | women residents of San Mateo County | $5000 | U.S. |
| Notah Begay III Scholarship Program | | graduating high school residents of New Mexico | $2000 | U.S. |
| Melbourne Alumnae Panhellenic Scholarship | | women who are attending a four-year college or | $2000 | U.S. |

|  |  |  |  |
|---|---|---|---|
|  | university in Florida |  |  |
| AAJA Seattle Northwest Journalists of Color Scholarship | Washington state high school seniors and undergraduate students | $2500 | U.S. |
| Denny's 'Hungry for Education' Scholarship | 16 years of age or older | $5000 | U.S. |
| Toigo MBA Fellowship | minority graduate students who are planning full-time MBA | $5000 | U.S. |
| Fredrikson & Byron Foundation Minority Scholarship Program | minority students who are in first year of law | $15000 | U.S. |

# Conclusion

Thank you for taking your time to download **Scholarships for Indian Students book.**

I believe the book has given you a deeper insight on the various types of scholarships and how you can make your application process a success. It is important to note that you might have the relevant qualifications but failure to read the instructions properly and be prepared in advance with the necessary documents before starting off the application process may lead to your application being rejected.

It is therefore advisable that you put into practice all the necessary measures in place so that you are able to submit an application that passes vetting process successfully in terms of accuracy of information, consistency and qualifications. Do not wait until the deadline is near as that is the time most applicants submit their forms.

I know you have found value in the information shared in this book and the best way you can benefit from the information is by making use of what you find relevant for your academic pursuit.

www.ingramcontent.com/pod-product-compliance
Lightning Source LLC
Chambersburg PA
CBHW071909290426
44110CB00013B/1333